THE
CONSCIOUSNESS
INDUSTRY

Hans Magnus Enzensberger

THE CONSCIOUSNESS INDUSTRY

On Literature, Politics and the Media

Selected & with a Postscript by
MICHAEL ROLOFF

A CONTINUUM BOOK   The Seabury Press · New York

English translation copyright © 1974 by The Seabury Press, Inc.
Editor: Michael Roloff
Design by Carol Basen
Printed in the United States of America

This selection appeared first in German in the following publications:

The Industrialization of the Mind (*Bewusstseins-Industrie*); *World Language of Modern Poetry* (*Weltsprache der Modernen Poesie*); *The Aporias of the Avant Garde* (*Die Aporien der Avantgarde*); *Poetry and Politics* (*Poesie und Politik*); in *Einzelheiten,* © Suhrkamp Verlag, Frankfurt, 1962. *Constituents of a Theory of the Media* (*Baukasten zu einer Theorie der Medien*); © Kursbuch Verlag, Berlin, 1971. *Commonplaces on the Newest Literature* (*Gemeinplätze zur neuesten Literatur*); © Kursbuch Verlag, Berlin, 1969. *Tourists of the Revolution* (*Revolutions-Tourismus*); © Kursbuch Verlag, Berlin, 1973.

The author extends grateful acknowledgment to *Partisan Review, New Left Review,* and *Modern Occasions Anthology* where, respectively, *Industrialization of the Mind, The Constituents of a Theory of the Media,* and *The Aporias of the Avant-Garde* first appeared in translation.

The author also extends grateful acknowledgment for the use of quoted material to the following publishers: Farrar, Straus & Giroux, Inc. for *A Trip to Hanoi* by Susan Sontag, © 1968 by Susan Sontag; Macmillan Publishing Co., Inc., for *Arrow in the Blue* by Arthur Koestler, © 1952 by Arthur Koestler; Alfred A. Knopf, Inc. and Pantheon Books, a Division of Random House, Inc., respectively, for *Return from the U.S.S.R.* by André Gide, © 1935 by Alfred A. Knopf, Inc., and *Report from a Chinese Village* by Jan Myrdal, © 1965 by Pantheon Books; Schocken Books, Inc., for "Josephine the Singer," reprinted by permission of Schocken Books, Inc., from *The Penal Colony* by Franz Kafka, copyright © 1948 by Schocken Books Inc.

LIBRARY OF CONGRESS CATALOGING IN PUBLICATION DATA
Enzensberger, Hans Magnus, 1929–
  The consciousness industry.

  (A Continuum book)
  CONTENTS: The industrialization of the mind.—The aporias of the avant garde.—The world language of modern poetry. [etc.]
  I. Roloff, Michael, ed. II. Title.
PT2609.N9C6   834'.9'14   73–17873
ISBN 0–8164–9185–2

Contents

THE
CONSCIOUSNESS
INDUSTRY

The industrialization of the mind

All of us, no matter how irresolute we are, like to think that we reign supreme in our own consciousness, that we are masters of what our minds accept or reject. Since the Soul is not much mentioned any more, except by priests, poets, and pop musicians, the last refuge a man can take from the catastrophic world at large seems to be his own mind. Where else can he expect to withstand the daily siege, if not within himself? Even under the conditions of totalitarian rule, where no one can fancy any more that his home is his castle, the mind of the individual is considered a kind of last citadel and hotly defended, though this imaginary fortress may have been long since taken over by an ingenious enemy.[1]

No illusion is more stubbornly upheld than the sovereignty of the mind. It is a good example of the impact of philosophy on people who ignore it; for the idea that men can "make up their minds" individually and by themselves is essentially derived from the tenets of bourgeois philosophy: secondhand Descartes, run-down Husserl, armchair idealism; and all it amounts to is a sort of metaphysical do-it-yourself.

We might do worse, I think, than dust off the admirably laconic statement which one of our classics made more than a century ago: "What is going on in our minds has always been, and will always be, a product of society." [2] This is a comparatively recent insight. Though it is valid for all human history ever since the division of labor came into being, it could not be formulated before the time of Karl Marx. In a society where communication was largely oral, the dependence of the pupil on the teacher, the disciple on the master, the flock on the priest was taken for granted. That the few thought and judged and decided for the many was a matter of course and not a matter for investigation. Medieval man was probably other-directed to an extent which our sociology would be at a loss to fathom. His mind was, to an enormous degree, fashioned and processed from "without." But the business of teaching and of indoctrination was perfectly straightforward and transparent—so transparent indeed that it became invisible as a problem. Only when the processes which shape our minds became opaque, enigmatic, inscrutable for the common man, only with the advent of industrialization, did the question of how our minds are shaped arise in earnest.

The mind-making industry is really a product of the last hundred years. It has developed at such a pace, and assumed such varied forms, that it has outgrown our understanding and our control. Our current discussion of the "media" seems to suffer from severe theoretical limitations. Newsprint, films, television, public relations tend to be evaluated separately, in terms of their specific technologies, conditions, and possibilities. Every new branch of the industry starts off a new crop of theories.[3] Hardly anyone seems to be aware of the phenomenon as a whole: the industrialization of the human mind. This is a process which cannot be understood by a mere examination of its machinery.

Equally inadequate is the term *cultural industry,* which has become common usage in Europe after World War II. It reflects, more than the scope of the phenomenon itself, the social status of those who have tried to analyze it: university professors and academic writers, people whom the power elite has relegated to the reservations of what passes as "cultural life" and who consequently have resigned themselves to bear the unfortunate name of cultural critics. In other words, they are certified as harmless; they are supposed to think in terms of *Kultur* and not in terms of power.

Yet the vague and insufficient name *cultural industry* serves to remind us of a paradox inherent in all media work. Consciousness, however false, can be induced and reproduced by industrial means, but it cannot be industrially produced. It is a "social product" made up by people: its origin is the dialogue. No industrial process can replace the persons who generate it. And it is precisely this truism of which the archaic term *culture* tries, however vainly, to remind us. The mind industry is monstrous and difficult to understand because it does not, strictly speaking, produce anything. It is an intermediary, engaged only in production's secondary and tertiary derivatives, in transmission and infiltration, in the fungible aspect of what it multiplies and delivers to the customer.

The mind industry can take on anything, digest it, reproduce it, and pour it out. Whatever our minds can conceive of is grist to its mill; nothing will leave it unadulterated: it is capable of turning any idea into a slogan and any work of the imagination into a hit. This is its overwhelming power, yet it is also its most vulnerable spot: it thrives on a stuff which it cannot manufacture by itself. It depends on the very substance it must fear most, and must suppress what it feeds on: the creative productivity of people. Hence the ambiguity of the term *cultural industry,* which takes at face value the claims of culture, in the ancient sense of the word, and the claims of an industrial process which has all but eaten it up. To insist on these claims would be naive; to criticize the industry from the vantage point of a "liberal education" and to raise comfortable outcries against its vulgarity will neither change it nor revive the dead souls of culture: it will merely help to fortify the ghettoes of educational programs and to fill the backward, highbrow section of the Sunday papers. At the same time, the indictment of the mind industry on purely esthetic grounds will tend to obscure its larger social and political meaning.

On the other extreme we find the ideological critics of the mind industry. Their attention is usually limited to its role as an instrument of straightforward or hidden political propaganda, and from the messages reproduced by it they try to distill the political content. More often than not, the underlying understanding of politics is extremely narrow, as if it were just a matter of taking sides in everyday contests of power. Just as in the case of the "cultural critic," this attitude cannot hope to catch up with the far-reaching effects of the industrialization of the mind, since it is a process which will abolish the distinction between private and public consciousness.

Thus, while radio, cinema, television, recording, advertising and public relations, new techniques of manipulation and propaganda, are being keenly discussed, each on its own terms, the mind industry, taken as a whole, is disregarded. Newsprint and publishing, its oldest and in many respects still its most interesting branch, hardly comes up for serious comment any longer, presumably because it lacks the appeal of technological novelty. Yet much of the analysis provided in Balzac's *Illusions Perdues* is as pertinent today as it was a hundred years ago, as any copywriter from Hollywood who happens to know the book will testify. Other, more recent branches of the industry still remain largely unexplored: fashion and industrial design, the propagation of established religions and of esoteric cults, opinion polls, simulation and, last but not least, tourism, which can be considered as a mass medium in its own right.

Above all, however, we are not sufficiently aware of the fact that the full deployment of the mind industry still lies ahead. Up to now it has not managed to seize control of its most essential sphere, which is education. The industrialization of instruction, on all levels, has barely begun. While we still indulge in controversies over curricula, school systems, college and university reforms, and shortages in the teaching professions, technological systems are being perfected which will make nonsense of all the adjustments we are now considering. The language laboratory and the closed-circuit TV are only the forerunners of a fully industrialized educational system which will make use of increasingly centralized programming and of recent advances in the study of learning. In that process, education will become a mass media, the most powerful of all, and a billion-dollar business.

Whether we realize it or not, the mind industry is growing faster than any other, not excluding armament. It has become the key industry of the twentieth century. Those who are concerned in the power game of today, political leaders, intelligence men, and revolutionaries, have very well grasped this crucial fact. Whenever an industrially developed country is occupied or liberated today, whenever there is a coup d'état, a revolution, or a counterrevolution, the crack police units, the paratroopers, the guerrilla fighters do not any longer descend on the main squares of the city or seize the centers of heavy industry, as in the nineteenth century, or symbolic sites like the royal palace; the new regime will instead take over, first of all, the radio and television stations, the telephone and telex exchanges, and the printing presses. And after having entrenched itself, it will, by and large, leave alone those who manage the public services and the manufacturing industries, at least in the beginning, while all the functionaries who run the mind industry will be immediately replaced. In such extreme situations the industry's key position becomes quite clear.

There are four conditions which are necessary to its existence; briefly, they are as follows:

1.) Enlightenment, in the broadest sense, is the philosophical prerequisite of the industrialization of the mind. It cannot get under way until the rule of theocracy, and with it people's faith in revelation and inspiration, in the Holy Book or the Holy Ghost as taught by the priesthood, is broken. The mind industry presupposes independent minds, even when it is out to deprive them of their independence; this is another of its paradoxes. The last theocracy to vanish has been Tibet; ever since, the philosophical condition is met with throughout the world.

2.) Politically, the industrialization of the mind presupposes the proclamation of human rights, of equality and liberty in particular. In Europe, this threshold has been passed by the French Revolution; in the Communist world, by the October Revolution; and in America, Asia, and Africa, by the wars of liberation from colonial rule. Obviously, the industry does not depend on the realization of these rights; for most people, they have never been more than a pretense, or at best, a distant promise. On the contrary, it is just the margin between fiction and reality which provides the mind industry with its theater of operations. Consciousness, both individual and social, has become a political issue only from the moment when the conviction arose in people's minds that everyone should have a say in his own destiny as well as in that of society at large. From the same moment any authority had to justify itself in the eyes of those it would govern; coercion alone would no longer do the trick; he who ruled must persuade, lay claim to people's minds and change them, in an industrial age, by every industrial means at hand.

3.) Economically, the mind industry cannot come of age unless a measure of primary accumulation has been achieved. A society which cannot provide the necessary surplus capital neither needs it nor can afford it. During the first half of the nineteenth century in Western Europe, and under similar conditions in other parts of the world, which prevailed until fairly recently, peasants and workers lived at a level of bare subsistence. During this stage of economic development the fiction that the working class is able to determine the conditions of its own existence is meaningless; the proletariat is subjected by physical constraint and undisguised force. Archaic methods of manipulation, as used by the school and by the church, the law and the army, together with old customs and conventions, are quite sufficient for the ruling minority to maintain its position during the earlier stages of industrial development. As soon as the basic industries have been firmly established and the mass production of consumer goods is beginning to reach out to the majority of the population, the ruling classes will face a dilemma. More sophisticated methods of production demand a constantly rising standard of education, not only for the privileged but also for the masses. The immediate compulsion which kept the working class "in their place" will slowly decrease. Working hours are reduced, and the standard of living rises. Inevitably, people will become aware of their own situation; they can now afford the luxury of having a mind of their own. For the first time, they become conscious of themselves in more than the most primitive and hazy sense of the word. In this process, enormous human energies are released, energies which inevitably threaten the established political and economic order. Today this revolutionary process can be seen at work in a great number of emergent nations, where it has long been artificially retarded by imperialist powers; in these countries the political, if not the economic conditions for the development of mind industries can be realized overnight.[4]

4.) Given a certain level of economic development, industrialization brings with it the last condition for the rise of a mind industry: the technology on which it depends. The first industrial uses of electricity were concerned with power and not with communications: the dynamo and the electrical motor preceded the amplifying valve and the film camera. There are economic reasons for this time lag: the foundations of radio, film, recording, television, and computing techniques could not be laid before the advent of the mass production of commodities and the general availability of electrical power.

In our time the technological conditions for the industrialization of the mind exist anywhere on the planet. The same cannot be said for the political and economic prerequisites; however, it is only a matter of time until they will be met. The process is irreversible. Therefore, all criticism of the mind industry which is abolitionist in its essence is inept and beside the point, since the idea of arresting and liquidating industrialization itself (which such criticism implies) is suicidal. There is a macabre irony to any such proposal, for it is indeed no longer a technical problem for our civilization to abolish itself. However, this is hardly what conservative critics have in mind when they complain about the loss of "values," the depravity of mass civilization and the degeneration of traditional culture by the media. The idea is, rather, to do away with all these nasty things, and to survive, as an elite of happy pundits, in the nicer comforts offered by a country house.

Nonetheless, the workings of the mind industry have been analyzed, in part, over and over again, sometimes with great ingenuity and insight. So far as the capitalist countries are concerned, the critics have leveled their attacks mainly against the newer media and commercial advertising. Conservatives and Marxists alike have been all too ready to deplore their venal side. It is an objection which hardly touches the heart of the matter. Apart from the fact that it is perhaps no more immoral to profit from the mass production of news or symphonies than from the mass production of soap and tires, objections of this kind overlook the very characteristics of the mind industry. Its more advanced sectors have long since ceased to sell any goods at all. With increasing technological maturity, the material substrata, paper or plastic or celluloid, tend to vanish. Only in the more old-fashioned offshoots of the business, as for example in the book trade, does the commodity aspect of the product play an important economic role. In this respect, a radio station has nothing in common with a match factory. With the disappearance of the material substratum the product becomes more and more abstract, and the industry depends less and less on selling it to its customers. If you buy a book, you pay for it in terms of its real cost of production; if you pick up a magazine, you pay only a fraction thereof; if you tune in on a radio or television program, you get it virtually free; direct advertising and political propaganda is something nobody buys—on the contrary, it is crammed down our throats. The products of the mind industry can no longer be understood in terms of a sellers' and buyers' market, or in terms of production costs: they are, as it were, priceless. The capitalist exploitation of the media is accidental and not intrinsic; to concentrate on their commercialization is to miss the point and to overlook the specific service which the mind industry performs for modern societies. This service is essentially the same all over the world, no matter how the industry is operated: under state, public, or private management, within a capitalist or a socialist economy, on a profit or nonprofit basis. The mind industry's main business and concern is not to sell its product: it is to "sell" the existing order, to perpetuate the prevailing pattern of man's domination by man, no matter who runs the society, and by what means. Its main task is to expand and train our consciousness—in order to exploit it.

Since "immaterial exploitation" is not a familiar concept,

it might be well to explain its meaning. Classical Marxism has defined very clearly the material exploitation to which the working classes have been subjected ever since the industrial revolution. In its crudest form, it is a characteristic of the period of the primary accumulation of capital. This holds true even for Socialist countries, as is evident from the example of Stalinist Russia and the early stages of the development of Red China. As soon as the bases of industrialization are laid, however, it becomes clear that material exploitation alone is insufficient to guarantee the continuity of the system. When the production of goods expands beyond the most immediate needs, the old proclamations of human rights, however watered down by the rhetoric of the establishment and however eclipsed by decades of hardship, famine, crises, forced labor, and political terror, will now unfold their potential strength. It is in their very nature that, once proclaimed, they cannot be revoked. Again and again, people will try to take them at their face value and, eventually, to fight for their realization. Thus, ever since the great declarations of the eighteenth century, every rule of the few over the many, however organized, has faced the threat of revolution. Real democracy, as opposed to the formal façades of parliamentary democracy, does not exist anywhere in the world, but its ghost haunts every existing regime. Consequently, all the existing power structures must seek to obtain the consent, however passive, of their subjects. Even regimes which depend on the force of arms for their survival feel the need to justify themselves in the eyes of the world. Control of capital, of the means of production, and of the armed forces is therefore no longer enough. The self-appointed elites who run modern societies must try to control people's minds. What each of us accepts or rejects, what we think and decide is now, here as well as in Vietnam, a matter of prime political concern: it would be too dangerous to leave these matters to ourselves. Material exploitation must camouflage itself in order to survive; immaterial exploitation has become its necessary corollary. The few cannot go on accumulating wealth unless they accumulate the power to manipulate the minds of the many. To expropriate manpower they have to expropriate the brain. What is being abolished in today's affluent societies, from Moscow to Los Angeles, is not exploitation, but our awareness of it.

It takes quite a lot of effort to maintain this state of affairs. There are alternatives to it. But since all of them would inevitably overthrow the prevailing powers, an entire industry is engaged in doing away with them, eliminating possible futures and reinforcing the present pattern of domination. There are several ways to achieve this end: on the one hand we find downright censorship, bans, and a state monopoly on all the means of production of the mind industry; on the other hand, economic pressures, systematic distribution of "punishment and reward," and human engineering can do the job just as well and much more smoothly. The material pauperization of the last century is followed and replaced by the immaterial pauperization of today. Its most obvious manifestation is the decline in political options available to the citizen of the most advanced nations: a mass of political nobodies, over whose heads even collective suicide can be decreed, is opposed by an ever-decreasing number of political moguls. That this state of affairs is readily accepted and voluntarily endured by the majority is the greatest achievement of the mind industry.

To describe its effects on present-day society is not, however, to describe its essence. The emergence of the textile industry has ruined the craftsman of India and caused widespread child labor in England, but these consequences do not necessarily follow from the existence of the mechanical loom. There is no more reason to suppose that the industrialization of the human mind must produce immaterial exploitation. It would even be fair to say that it will eventually, by its own logic, do away with the very results it has today. For this is the most fundamental of all its contradictions: in order to obtain consent, you have to grant a choice, no matter how marginal and deceptive; in order to harness the faculties of the human mind, you have to develop them, no matter how narrowly and how deformed. It may be a measure of the overwhelming power of the mind industry that none of us can escape its influence. Whether we like it or not, it enlists our participation in the system as a whole. But this participation may very well veer, one day, from the passive to the active, and turn out to threaten the very order it was supposed to uphold. The mind industry has a dynamic of its own which it cannot arrest, and it is not by chance but by necessity that in this movement there are currents which run contrary to its present mission of stabilizing the status quo. A corollary of its dialectical progress is that the mind industry, however closely supervised in its individual operations, is never completely controllable as a whole. There are always leaks in it, cracks in the armor; no administration will ever trust it all the way.[5]

In order to exploit people's intellectual, moral, and political faculties, you have got to develop them first. This is, as we have seen, the basic dilemma faced by today's media. When we turn our attention from the industry's consumers to its producers, the intellectuals, we find this dilemma aggravated and intensified. In terms of power, of course, there can be no question as to who runs the business. Certainly it is not the intellectuals who control the industrial establishment, but the establishment which controls them. There is precious little chance for the people who are productive to take over their means of production: this is just what the present structure is designed to prevent. However, even under present circumstances, the relationship is not without a certain ambiguity, since there is no way of running the mind industry without enlisting the services of at least a minority of men who can create something. To exclude them would be self-defeating. Of course, it is perfectly possible to use the whole stock of accumulated original work and have it adapted, diluted, and processed for media use, and it may be well to remember that much of what purports to be new is in fact derivative. If we examine the harmonic and melodic structure of any popular song hit, it will most likely turn out to employ inventions of serious composers centuries ago. The same is true of the dramaturgical clichés of mediocre screenplays: watered down beyond recognition, they repeat traditional patterns taken from the drama and the novel of the past. In the long run, however, the parasitic use of inherited work is not sufficient to nourish the industry. However large a stock, you cannot sell out forever without replenishment; hence the need "to make it new," the media's dependence on men capable of innovation, in other words, on potential troublemakers. It is inherent in the process of creation that there is no way to predict its results. Consequently, intellectuals are, from the point of view of any power structure bent on its own perpetuation, a security risk. It takes consummate skill to "handle" them and to neutralize their subversive influence. All sorts of techniques, from the crudest to the most sophisticated, have been developed to this end: physical threat, blacklisting, moral and economic pressure on the one hand, overexposure, star-cult, co-optation into the power elite on the other, are the extremes of a whole gamut of manipulation. It would be worthwhile to write a manual analyzing these techniques. They have one thing in common, and that is that they offer short-term, tactical answers to a problem which, in principle, cannot be resolved. This is an industry which has to rely, as its primary source, on the very minorities with whose elimination it is entrusted: those whose aim it is to invent and produce *alternatives*. Unless it succeeds in exploiting and manipulating its producers, the mind industry cannot hope to exploit and manipulate its consumers. On the level of production, even more than on the level of consumption, it has to deal with partners who are potential enemies. Engaged in the proliferation of human consciousness, the media proliferate their own contradictions.

Criticism of the mind industry which fails to recognize its central ambiguities is either idle or dangerous. It is a measure of their limitations that many media critics never seem to reflect on their own position, just as if their work were not itself a part of what it criticizes. The truth is that no one can nowadays express any opinion at all without making use of the industry, or rather, without being used by it.[6]

Anyone incapable of dialectical thinking is doomed as soon as he starts grappling with this subject. He will be trapped to a point where even retreat is no longer possible. There are many who feel revolted at the thought of entering a studio or negotiating with the slick executives who run the networks. They detest, or profess to detest, the very machinery of the industry, and would like to withdraw into some abode of refinement. Of course, no such refuge really exists. The seemingly exclusive is just another, slightly more expensive line of styling within the same giant industrial combine.

Let us rather try to draw the line between intellectual integrity and defeatism. To opt out of the mind industry, to refuse any dealings with it may well turn out to be a reactionary course. There is no hermitage left for those whose job is to speak out and to seek innovation. Retreat from the media will not even save the intellectual's precious soul from corruption. It might be a better idea to enter the dangerous game, to take and calculate our risks. Instead of innocence, we need determination. We must know very precisely the monster we are dealing with, and we must be continually on our guard to resist the overt or subtle pressures which are brought to bear on us.

The rapid development of the mind industry, its rise to a key position in modern society, has profoundly changed the role of the intellectual. He finds himself confronted with new threats and new opportunities. Whether he knows it or not, whether he likes it or not, he has become the accomplice of a huge industrial complex which depends for its survival on him, as he depends on it for his own. He must try, at any cost, to use it for his own purposes, which are incompatible with the purposes of the mind machine. What it upholds he must subvert. He may play it crooked or straight, he may win or lose the game; but he would do well to remember that there is more at stake than his own fortune.

Translated by the author.

The aporias of
the avant-garde

To count himself a member of the avant-garde has for several lifetimes now been the privilege of everyone who covers empty surfaces with paint or sets down letters or notes on paper. Not everyone has availed himself of this opportunity. Whoever undauntedly sticks the label *avant-gardist* on an author like Franz Kafka is already seduced into negligence by that mouthful of a word; it would have stuck in Kafka's craw. Neither Marcel Proust nor William Faulkner, neither Bertolt Brecht nor Samuel Beckett—none of them, as far as we know, has invoked that vocable, which nowadays, to be sure, every laundry list lays claim to, but on whose meaning, as if it were settled once and for all, hardly anyone of the crowd who mouth it stops to reflect.

This is true of the partisans of the avant-garde no less than of its enemies. They differ in their judgments but not in their premises. Both sides help themselves uncritically to a critical concept that struck it rich in Paris over a hundred years ago, and has since passed for a touchstone of which it has not been expected or demanded that it undergo a test itself. The minds that it separates from one another have a way of lapsing into a permanent debate whose beginnings are lost in a mist and whose end can be held off ad libitum. Names and catch phrases change; the schema remains the same. Since Swift's *Full and True Account of the Battle Between the Ancient and the Modern Books* (1710), this controversy has lost some of its originality and brilliance; what remains is that modest abstraction for which, all along, it was willing to settle. The cast-iron stances of the contenders, no matter on which side, are of a depressing innocuousness; they remind one of the figures of middle-class family drama to whose antiquated conflict between father and son they would reduce the march of history. Commonplaces like the ones about the impetuous youngster whose ears will yet be pinned back, about the excesses of youth and the wisdom of maturity, and about the enlightened traditionalism of age that looks back with a wink on its own rebellious past are characteristic of the entire sphere of such discussions, with their lack of a sense of history. Unhistoric, not merely hackneyed, is the blind trust they are happy to put in the threadbare concept of generations, quite as if it were the life of the arts, rather than that of trichinae, that is subject to the biological law of the life cycle; or as if the content of a hymn by Hölderlin or a play by Brecht could be read off the author's "vintage." Whoever distinguishes between old and new, or old and young, in such comfortable fashion, agrees by his very choice of criteria with the philistines. To him, the simplest dialectical propositions must remain inaccessible. That the durability of works is always determined only by their immanence in today's creation, which simultaneously devours and rejuvenates them, remains unfathomed, indeed unfathomable, even though this insight could be gleaned at the starting point of all European thought: "The old, veering round, becomes the new, and the latter, veering back, the former." The statement is to be found in Heraclitus.

The argument between the partisans of the old and those of the new is unendurable, not so much because it drags on endlessly, unresolved and irresoluble, but because its schema itself is worthless. The choice that it invites is not only banal, it is a priori factitious. The semblance of a timeless symmetry with which it surrounds itself is invalidated by history, which has so far overtaken every unhistoric position and given it the lie. For no sooner do the arts enter the gravitational field of totalitarianism than the harmless tug of war about the avant-garde, or rather what passes for it, assumes murderous traits. The symmetry of the old and the new, that timeless mirror image, is brutally broken in two, and its real substratum becomes manifest. No avant-garde has thus far called

opponents. The "healthy forces
hat have persistently sanctioned
s on publishing, indeed murder,
cism to other means; they pur-
the political conditions permit,
or rather command them to talk of a breach.

Only when it has come to that (but it has always come to
that on the other side of the fence) do the categories of "progressive" and "reactionary" in the arts come into their own.
To be sure, they are scarcely less questionable and shabby
than those of the Old and the New; moreover, so many card-
sharps have been operating with them that there are indelible
black marks against them on the books. Nevertheless, they can
lay claim to their historicity; they are not suited to the analysis of biological but of historic processes. So long as somewhere
in the world esthetic questions are settled by force—so long,
indeed, as such a procedure can be reckoned with as a real
possibility—they are indispensable; in other words, everywhere and for an unforeseeable length of time. They require
no metaphysical foundation. Their usefulness is simply and
solely heuristic.[1] They require, therefore, constant reappraisal;
like every indispensable device, they imperil the user as soon
as he relies on them blindly. What most profoundly distinguishes the progressive attitude from every reactionary one is
precisely its relation to doubt. The readiness to revise all
solidified theses, to examine endlessly its own premises, is the
essence of all progressive criticism. Reactionary criticism, on
the contrary, considers itself, so to speak, naturally and ever-
lastingly in the right. It is exempt from reflecting on its presuppositions. As complaisantly as it adapts its judgment, from
case to case, to the nature of the powers that be, as unshakably
has it established what is to be considered beautiful, sane, and
constructive.

Only after coming into power does it reveal its brutal coun-
tenance. Until then it operates in the underbrush of con-
venticles, on the unsurveyable terrain of textbooks and "education in the arts"; in the open, it observes certain precau-
tions. Under democratic conditions, reactionary criticism sees

itself constrained to deny its own existence. It even admits tacitly to its canon of imperishables what it previously denigrated: the moment a modern work is no longer new, no longer risky, it is claimed as a "contemporary classic" by that very criticism which for decades tried in vain to strike it dead with its "rigid yardstick." Once annexed to the heritage that must be preserved, it is truly deprived of its life, that is, removed from criticism and exhibited as an embalmed holy relic. Whatever he cannot lick, the reactionary critic will join, and even thinks thereby to demonstrate his magnanimity. As long as he cannot enforce his doctrine with police assistance, he finds himself willing even to sign a truce and passes himself off as a mediator and man of common sense who stands "above the press of things." Social pluralism becomes, for the time being, an esthetic pillow; in the dark of freedom, all cats are gray. Every work has its justification along with every other one, trash "complements" the masterpiece, and with the obligingness of all judgments the critical faculty itself is made to vanish by sleight of hand.

Neutrality of this ilk, which likes to answer to the name of "openmindedness," condemns itself. At the first sign that esthetic questions are about to be adjudicated by the power of the state, it flaps over into what it has secretly been all along. In the face of a rule of terror, whether exercised by a Goebbels or a Zhdanov, there can be no tolerance; which, for reactionary criticism, means that tolerance for the victims of that terror can be dispensed with. Such criticism rests untroubled on its certitudes as long as it sees to it that the yardsticks of its Beckmesserdom are always calibrated according to regulation.

The prescriptions are always the same: "The emphasis must be placed on questions pertaining to a world view." The work of art is nothing in itself; it functions merely as the "representative" of the currently demanded *"Weltanschauung,"* which it must "adequately reproduce." "What matters is not the specific, artistically formal manner of writing, but this stand in terms of an ultimate world view." Opportunism that makes common cause with the stronger battalions is candidly appealed to: "Affiliation with the determinant tendencies of the times, which, sooner or later, will be the ruling ones," is what the writer must seek, placing himself "on the ground" designated to him by reactionary criticism. He is thus given the "concrete plumb line" by which he can hang himself, and "the justified, world-historic optimism, so extraordinarily fruitful for art" will then come about on its own. The arts are there to supply "lifelike realism" and "all-embracing positivism" and "to fashion man's future from within." "The will and aptitude for the creation of such a positive, new reality" facilitate "the choice between social health and sickness." "From that there follows"—verbatim!—"such a heightening of the watchtower" that it can no longer be doubted what sort of strait jacket the watchman intends for the arts; the avant-garde, whatever that term means to him, is "decadent," "perverse," "cynical," "nihilistic," and "sickly." This vocabulary will be well remembered from the *Völkische Beobachter,* and that the state of mind it expresses has not died out in our land is demonstrated by every second glance into the newspapers that appear between Bonn and Passau. The quoted phrases did not, however, sprout from fascist dung; they were not culled from the *Neues Deutschland,* either. The man who wrote them passes for the most intelligent, distinguished, and courageous literary critic whom Communism can point to anywhere; they appear in Georg Lukács's book, *Against Misunderstood Realism,*[2] which could not be published on the other side of the Elbe, for to the cultural police that have the final word there it seemed still not reactionary enough. To be sure, Lukács objects—in a language that, probably unjustly, claims to derive from Schiller and Goethe—to the "ever more pronounced stepping-into-the-foreground of the pathological" in literature, but he does not opt for the therapy that customarily follows on such pronouncements and consists of liquidating the patient. Lukács does not by any means reach for his gun when he hears the word *culture.* He has kept within him a remnant of that bad conscience that the most intelligent "representatives" of reactionary criticism bring to it as a dowry. It stirs in vain.

The "artistic striving" of such criticism does not manifest itself only in that its language, under whatever party insignia, gets tattered and rotten. This criticism can dispense even with the knowledge of what it defames. The goat turned gardener need not concern itself with botany. It separates herbs from weeds with its horns. What passes for healthy is most likely to be the mediocre: Theodore Dreiser, Sinclair Lewis, Norman Mailer, Romain Rolland, and Roger Martin du Gard are for Lukács the quintessence of modern literature. To what unhappy misconception Thomas and Heinrich Mann may owe their appearance on this roster of those given a clean bill of health remains inscrutable. Sickly and decadent, however, in contradistinction to the apple-cheeked author of *The Black Swan,* are Dos Passos and Beckett, Montherlant and Kafka, Proust and Jens Rehn, Koeppen and Jünger, Gide and Faulkner—about as nonsensical a collocation of names as could possibly be conceived.[3] Tonsure is administered with the self-same unclean comb to heads that, for content and quality, for style and provenance, simply cannot be compared. Lukács calls this pocket comb "avant-gardism"—naturally without taking the trouble to analyze the term.[4] Nor have Hanns Johst and Will Vesper made the art of discrimination any harder for themselves.

Neither Western nor Eastern exponents of such criticism, on whatever bastions they may ply their trade, are competent to criticize the avant-garde. Their verdict about what is healthy or sick—about the meritorious or the degenerate—must be implemented by the police, or it remains without significance. With every one of their anathemas, they attest to their lack of authority.

In the face of their censure, whose aim is nothing other than censorship, solidarity goes without saying. Every work deserves to be defended against its suppressors: this tenet precedes all esthetic probing, and even the most superfluous "experiment" may have recourse to it. A criticism that considers itself progressive must weigh all the more carefully its rights and duties precisely as regards the most advanced production. If it is content with turning the verdicts of the culture wardens upside down, it thereby makes them seem only more justified. Whoever denies the bailiffs of unjust power their competence cannot simultaneously vindicate himself by reference to their pronouncements. Solidarity can be valid in the arts only so long as it is not used as a carte blanche. What proclaims itself the avant-garde is by no means immune to criticism. There is much evidence for this term's having become nowadays a talisman, which is to make its wearers proof against all objections and to intimidate perplexed reviewers. What is most revealing is that the term, to this day, has not been analyzed. Those who would be happiest to eradicate it have never specially concerned themselves with what the avant-garde actually is. That is understandable. What is queerer is that its followers have hardly contributed more to the definition of that which they admire than have its foes. The concept *avant-garde* is in need of elucidation.

Under that catchword, there appears in all [German] dictionaries, in token of its military derivation, a pair of crossed daggers. Older works of reference do not even recognize the figurative meaning:

Avant-garde, advance guard, vanguard, that segment of a marching troop which the latter (the main body) sends some distance forward. . . . An a. subdivides itself frontward into ever smaller divisions, down to the spearhead marching at the very forefront. Each of these subdivisions serves the purpose of gaining for the larger one following it more security and time. . . . The flung-out smaller divisions must govern themselves as to their movement according to the larger ones that follow them.[5]

The transfer of this strategic concept to the arts was first effected in the fifties of the past century in France. The metaphor has since dislodged and obscured the original sense of the term; it must, however, accept the fact of being taken at its word. The objection that it wasn't meant that way comes ready to hand but does not matter. The figure of speech preserves what its users have forgotten; analysis merely brings to light what presuppositions it drags along. The concept of the avant-garde is, like the word itself, a composite.

Its first component poses no conundrum. The field in which the avant-garde moves is history. The preposition *avant,* conceived spatially in the technical military sense, returns in the metaphor to its original temporal significance. The arts are regarded not as historically unvarying activities of mankind or as an arsenal of timelessly extant "cultural goods" but as a continually advancing process, as a work in progress, in which every single production participates.

Now, this process has a single direction. Only that makes it possible to differentiate advance guard, main body, and rear guard. Not all works are equally far "forward," and it is by no means a matter of indifference which position they occupy. The pathos of the concept feeds on the notion that the place at the spearhead of the process distinguishes a work, endows it with a rating denied other works. What is being compared is not really present performance with the past. To be sure, the avant-garde metaphor does not exclude the dull and inferior view that whatever came earlier can, for that very reason, be thrown on the junk heap. But it cannot be reduced to vulgar worship of the latest thing. Included in the concept is the nonsimultaneity of the simultaneous: precursors and stragglers are, at every moment of the process, simultaneously present. External and internal contemporaneity fall apart. The *en avant* of the avant-garde would, as it were, realize the future in the present, anticipate the course of history.

This conception has its justification in the fact that art without a moment of anticipation cannot even be thought of. It is contained in the very process of creation: the work is preceded by the design. The design, the project, does not disappear in its realization. Every work of art, and the masterwork in particular, has in it something unfinished; indeed, this necessary residue makes up its durability: only when it fades does the work fade with it. An inkling of it is the prerequisite of all productivity. The idea of fame has its roots here. It has always been the notion of posthumous fame, not to be compared with mere celebrity during one's lifetime. Only subsequent generations can fulfill the work of art that juts, uncompleted, into the future; only they can, so to speak, redeem anticipation through fame. The works of antiquity were created in this confidence. It is stated explicitly in a widespread literary *topos:* the poet's apostrophe to posterity.

With the development of historical consciousness, this faith in posterity begins to decline. No doubt, there opens before any work, even the least significant, a prospect of a new immortality: everything can, indeed must, be preserved in mankind's memory—but as a "memorial," as a relic. That brings up the question of surpassability. Eternal survival in the museum is being bought with the prospect that henceforth the march of history can stride across everything without extinguishing it. Everyone becomes aware of the process of steady advance, and this awareness, in turn, becomes the motor that accelerates the process. The arts no longer find protection in their future: it confronts them as a threat and makes them dependent on itself. Faster and faster, history devours the works it brings to fruition.

From now on, the arts are cognizant of their own historicity as a stimulant and a threat, but this change of consciousness is not all there is to it. The triumph of capitalism turns it into a hard economic fact: it brings the work of art into the market place. It thus enters into a state of competition not only with other merchandise but also with every other work of art. The historic contest for future recognition becomes a competition for present purchase. The mechanics of the market imitates the devouring course of history on a smaller scale: it is geared to a rapid turnover in accord with the scant breath and crude eye of planned economy. The anticipatory moment of art is cut down to a mere speculation; its future is charted like that of stocks and shares. Historic movement is observed, comprehended, and discounted—a market trend upon whose correct prediction economic success depends. In the long run, however, the consciousness industry does not content itself with merely letting its augurs survey the market place of the arts. It attempts to insure itself against changes in the weather by creating it. If it does not exactly invent tomorrow's trend, it certainly proclaims and promotes it. The future of the work of art is sold before it has even occurred. What is steadily being offered for sale is, as in other industries, next year's model. But this future has not only always begun; it is also, when tossed out into the market, always already past. Tomorrow's esthetic product offered for sale today proves, the day after tomorrow, a white elephant and, no longer sellable, wanders into the archives in the hope of the possibility that, ten years later, it might still be palmed off as the object of a sentimental revival. Thus the work of art too is subject to the industrial procedure of built-in obsolescence; its afterlife is immediately cashed in on and cashiered; indeed, it is transmogrified, by way of publicity, into a forelife, which the work inherits before it even appears on the scene. Its afterlife is factory-made. The proposition concerning the nonsimultaneity of the simultaneous is realized by training the clientele to become a vanguard that insists on being served the newest thing and demands the future, so to speak, as consumer goods.

As suppliers of this industry, writers, painters, composers assume, economically speaking, the traits of employees. They must "keep in step with the times" and always nose out the competitors. To keep in the forefront, they must not "fail to connect." This explains why fifty-year-olds let themselves be described as young authors. Such an economic disposition obviously invites contemptible maneuvering. It gives rise to an avant-garde as bluff, as escape forward, with which the main body, for fear of being left behind, falls in. The type of the fellow traveler who would like to pass for a forerunner becomes prominent; in the rush for the future, every ram fancies himself the bellwether. The man on the treadmill remains unremittingly the object of a process that he thinks he is, as subject, in control of.

These economic consequences, however, merely reveal an aporia that is posited with the very concept of an avant-garde in the arts. What is questionable is not just its commercial exploitation but also the very *en avant* with which the avant-garde presents itself. For just who, other than the avant-garde itself, is to determine what at any given time is "to the fore" remains an open question. "The flung-out smaller divisions must govern themselves as to their movement," if we may trust the Brockhaus, "according to the larger ones that follow them"; but that means, as soon as a spatial movement is translated into a temporal one, governing themselves according to an unknown body.

Of course, it is possible to verify without much trouble that there exists at all times a rear guard. It coincides without fail with what reactionary criticism recommends as healthy. Its physiognomy can be described down to its minutest traits, for in them it is only the all-too-familiar that epigonously recurs. An extreme, very-well-explored example is the popular novel, which always reiterates older, exhausted patterns in distorted fashion. This does not actually devaluate what previous epochs have produced; devaluated, rather, are the suppliers of this rear guard, which likes to justify itself—but always unjustly —with reference to tradition. Its unassuming, petty bourgeois wing is shielded from every objection by its stupidity; in Communist countries, it enjoys state protection; in neocapitalist society, it supplies, hardly observed by the public eye, the proletariat, which, by universal demand, has been rechristened "lower middle class." How this majority of the population is being provided for, without dissension, with fifth-hand esthetics, can be studied in the catalogs of the large department stores and mail-order houses. At the forefront of this inarticulate rear guard is to be placed that "elevated" group, which consists of "culture bearers." Its speciality is the aristocratic gesture with which it purports to "attend to spiritual interests" and defend "values"; its shadowboxing with modernity, of many decades' standing, needs no elucidation, and its points of view have become known *ad nauseam*.

On the other hand, it is not possible to discern a vantage point from which one could determine what is avant-garde and what isn't. All the efforts of the consciousness industry to detect a trend in the historic movement of the arts and elevate its prognostications to the level of a dictate misfire as speculation; at best, it is by chance that it scores any bull's-eyes. The actual process puts to shame not only the impotent attempts of the Communists to plan it but also the cleverer endeavors of capitalist economy, which would steer it by means of advertising and market manipulations. All that can be affirmed is what *was* "out front," not what *is* there. The work of Kleist or Kafka remained invisible to their contemporaries not because they refused to "go with the times" but because they went with the times. This does not mean that, in the arts, what contains futurity must go unrecognized. The notion of the unrecognized has, in any case, taken on an old-fashioned coloring, ever since the capacity of the reproducing apparatus has become greater than existing production, and since, consequently, anything at all that anyone writes or paints is indiscriminately and suspiciously publicized. That in this way every work—let alone one that anticipates the future—is done justice to cannot for a moment be entertained; there is no authority before which such justice can be pleaded or, like a tariff regulation, implemented. Where the word *avant-garde* is being construed in the present tense, a doctrinaire formulation results. Whoever becomes rigid about objective necessity, the demands of the medium, and compulsory evolution is already in the wrong. Every such doctrine relies on the method of extrapolation: it projects lines into the unknown. Such a procedure, however, will not get even at a political or economic process, because it is applicable only to linear, not to dialectical operations, to say nothing of an esthetic process, which can be apprehended through no prognosis, not even a statistical one, because its characteristics are determined by leaps. Their spontaneous appearance defies any theory of futurity.

The model according to which the concept of the avant-garde orients itself is invalid. The forward march of the arts through history is conceived of as a linear, perspicuous, and surveyable movement in which everyone can himself determine his place, at the forefront or with the hangers-on. What is overlooked is that this movement leads from the known into the unknown; that, therefore, only the stragglers can indicate where they are. Nobody knows what is up front, least of all he who has reached unknown territory. Against this uncertainty there is no insurance. Only someone willing to suffer the consequences of error can get involved with the future. The *avant* of the avant-garde contains its own contradiction: it can be marked out only a posteriori.

The metaphor of the avant-garde, however, contains not only temporal but also sociological determinants. These are expressed in the second component of the compound term.

Guards is the name given, other than to the bodyguards of princes, in many armies, to elite troops distinguished by excellent supplies and especially brilliant uniforms (cf. *Elite*); they are usually garrisoned in capitals and royal residential towns. Guard means originally an enclosure. . . . Napoleon I must be considered the actual creator of the g. Tradition puts into the mouth of its commander, General Cambronne (to be sure, without foundation), the saying, "The guard dies, but does not surrender." [6]

Every guard is a collective; that is the first thing that can be deduced from this word. First the group, and only then the individual, whose decisions are of no consequence in the undertakings of the guard, unless he be its leader. For every guard is most rigorously divided into the one who issues the commands and passwords of the day and the many who receive them, pass them on, and obey them. What all who belong to it have in common is discipline. Without dictates and regulations, it cannot manage. To abide by them is not always easy, but it does relieve the member of the guard of many worries. Along with his freedom, he delegates to the collective body doubt, fear, and insecurity; he feels surer about his cause, which is no longer his concern but that of the whole. The protection that the guard vouchsafes is enjoyed, in the first place, by the guard itself. The guardsman has not only duties but also rights—to be exact, prerogatives. To belong to the guard is a distinction. It is an exclusive league of men; the enclosure keeps others out. Every guard, and so too the avant-garde, considers itself an elite. It is proud not only of being ahead of and further on than the others but also of belonging to a distinguished minority.

The guard's vocation is combat. In it, and only in it, does the guard prove its worth. Not productivity but contest is its *raison d'être:* it is always militant. Here the transfer of the concept to the arts leads into some difficulties. What adversary does the vanguard expect to encounter on the terrain of history if it alone, and nobody else, operates in, or into, the future? What enemy army could it meet there? Enemies should not be lacking to anyone who forsakes the safe, allegedly so "healthy" grounds of mediocrity; but these adversaries seem to be located in back of him rather, and aside from the fact that he will not exactly see his purpose in life as fighting the likes of them, it just will not jibe with the idea of a guard that its only foe should be the tail of that very column it has the privilege of leading.

The concept of the avant-garde was applied not only to the arts but also, over half a century later, more felicitously and sensibly to politics. In 1919, Lenin defined the Communist Party as the avant-garde of the proletariat.[7] This formula became part of the international Communist vocabulary.[8] It pinpoints what the avant-garde metaphor sociologically comprehends, or rather, uncomprehendingly drags along. The role played by Sorel's concept of an elite in the development of Lenin's theories is well known. Very much in Sorel's sense, the party is to Lenin a strictly organized, elite combat unit, where absolute internal discipline is a matter of course; no less obviously, it is entitled to a privileged position vis-à-vis the outsiders, the mass of non-party members. Here the avant-garde metaphor is thought out with sharp consistency down to its last detail. At one point only does the figurative meaning diverge from the literal one: the Communist avant-garde need not "govern itself as to its movement" according to the main body, but conversely, it is at the same time the general staff according to whose plans the entire operation must proceed: it enforces the dictatorship not only *of* but also *over* the proletariat. Understandably, if the revolution is to be "carried out" in the name of the majority but against its will, what is required is not so much muses as a bodyguard. In all other particulars, however, the Communist concept of an avant-garde is strictly relevant. What is "forward" is determined once and for all by an infallible doctrine, and the adversary at whom the vanguard action is directed is established and really there.

Beside Lenin's well-defined application of it to politics, the concept of the avant-garde in the arts appears to be somewhat confused. Least convincing is its collective trait. Clearly, a historic process has many collaborators, so many that it would be ridiculous to speculate about just how many individuals at a given period "constitute" a literature. But as much as every literature is a collective effort, as little is it to be visualized as a troop organized along disciplinary lines and sworn to a doctrine. Whoever participates in it enters forthwith into a direct relationship with the process as a whole; he can consign his freedom and risks to no group outside of himself.

The avant-garde metaphor does not contain the slightest reference to a revolutionary or even rebellious intent. Nothing is more glaring than this lack. Yet so far every group that made use of the concept, in the arts as in politics, viewed itself as a *Fronde* and proclaimed the overthrow of existing conditions. No avant-garde program but protests the inertia of the merely extant and promises to burst esthetic and political bonds, throw off established rule, liberate suppressed energies. Freedom, gained through revolution, is heralded by all avant-garde movements. It is to this claim, which it does not even express, rather than to its future-orientedness, rather than to its promise to form an elite, that the concept of the avant-garde owes its emotional appeal. This aspect too was thought out more acutely and thoroughly by Lenin than by all the writers and painters. From what the Communist avant-garde would free its partisans and everybody else is made clear beyond any doubt; its revolutionary character will not be denied by its worst enemy. By contrast, it remains vague and blurry just what freedom the manifestoes of the artistic avant-garde have in mind and what the word *revolution,* frequently though it may appear in them, is supposed to mean there. All too often these manifestoes sound both grandiloquent and innocuous, as if they had no other concern than to scare off bourgeois conventions, which, in any case, are nothing more than ghosts. The cry for absolute freedom rings peculiar when the question involved is whether or not fish may be eaten with a knife. The propensity for revolutionary rhetoric may reveal the surface nakedness of the avant-garde; it does, how-

ever, cover up its central aporias. Only where it ruthlessly
formulates its aims and methods, as with Lenin, do these
aporias become apparent.

In much the same way as Communism in society, the avant-
garde in the arts would enforce freedom in doctrinaire fashion.
Just like the Party, it believes itself to have taken, as a revolutionary elite, which is to say as a collective, a lease on the
future. It disposes with the indefinable in the most definite
manner. It arbitrarily dictates what will be valid tomorrow
and, simultaneously, submits, disciplined and will-less, to the
commands of a future of its very own contriving. It proclaims
as its goal total freedom, and surrenders, unresisting, to the historic process, which is to relieve it of that self-same freedom.

These aporias lie in the concept *avant-garde* itself. They can
be verified empirically in all groups that have had recourse
to it, but they have never become more flagrantly apparent
than in that which today exhibits itself as the avant-garde: in
tachism, in *art informel,* and in monochrome painting; in
serial and electronic music; in the so-called concrete poetry;
and in the literature of the beat generation.[9] These movements have in common the more or less obstreperously announced conviction of being "out front," their doctrinaire
bias, and their collective state. That their names have become,
in the course of a few years, catchwords, indeed trademarks,
stems not merely from their accord with the consciousness industry; these terms were launched with premeditation as handy
slogans. Avant-gardism, nowadays, is brought into currency
overnight as coin of the realm. All the more reason for examining the coinage a little more closely.

It is to Jack Kerouac, the supreme commander of the Beat-
nik sect, canonized by his partisans as Holy Jack, that we owe
the following maxim, which he posited in his "Credo" together with a "List of Indispensable Remedies" for the writer:
"Be always idiotically absentminded!" The sentence can serve
as motto for the current mass productions of tachism, *art informel,* action painting, concrete poetry *in toto,* as well as
for a large part of the latest music. Kerouac goes on: "My
style is based on spontaneous get-with-it, unrepressed word-
slinging. . . . Push aside literary, grammatical and syntactic

obstacles! Strike as deep as you can strike! Visionary spasms shoot through the breast. You are at all times a genius." [10] To be sure, the avant-garde bares its breast with so much naiveté (even if false) only between New York and San Francisco. The harmless simplicity with which it proclaims barbarism has a downright endearing effect in contrast to its European counterpart. Here indeterminacy expresses itself in a petrified academic jargon that dishes out delirium like a seminar report: the proffered texts form "a system of words, letters or signs, which obtain their meaning only through the personal contribution of the reader. . . . They are arbitrarily disposed in the sixteen directions of the quadratic square and aligned in a chance sequence . . . they possess stringency only through the swirls of motion and the assent they evoke in the reader . . . when carried through with rigorous consistency, they debouch into the black stone, the last standstill, as the no-further-enhanceable complex motion. Are, thereby, concrete form, uninterruptedly centered point, objective duration in nature (as materia-l *sine qua non*) guess whyyyy." [11]

That reads like a translation of Kerouac's catechism into occidental culture-gibberish. The translator keeps strictly to the prescriptions of the original, which, to be sure, is garnished with eruditional flotsam, but to whose intellectual exiguity he remains absolutely faithful. Mobility raised to an end in itself reappears as "swirls of the no-further-enhanceable complex motion," and the "visionary spasms" turn into "the black stone guess whyyyy." In both cases, mystification demands "carrying through with rigorous consistency," and the precept "Be always idiotically absentminded" lays claim to stringency. An idea of the possibilities this avant-garde opens up may be gleaned from the following "text":[12]

```
ra ra ra ra ra ar ra ra ra ra ar ar er ir
ra ra ra ra ar ar ar ka ra ra ar ar ar er
ra ra ra ar ar ar ak af ka ra ar ar ar ra
ra ra ar ar ar ak af ab af ka ar ar ra ra
ra ar ar ar ak af ab af ab af ak ra ra ra
```

This result does not stand in isolation. Works of the same stamp are available in such quantities that it would be unjust to name the begetter of the specimen, even though he has already made a bit of a name for himself with his output. Since, however, it is hardly distinguishable from the outpourings of his companions, what should, rather, be considered the author, insofar as this word still applies, is the collective: in such texts the guard brings itself into being. It can be seen at a glance (and this in itself justifies the reproduction of a specimen) that the sociological aporias of the avant-garde are repeated in these texts quite accurately on the formal level; indeed, they perfectly consume themselves in their reproduction. Indeterminacy appears as doctrine, retrogression as progress. The milkman's bill masquerades as inspired madness, quietism as action, chance as prescription.

That these characteristics apply not only to "concrete poetry" and the literature of the beat generation but also to the self-declared avant-garde in all the arts is demonstrated by an international album in which it draws its self-portrait and which purports to be "at once account, documentation, analysis and program." It contains a list of basic concepts and categories, which are supposed to be equally valid for literature and painting, music and sculpture, film and architecture (insofar as such distinctions are still permissible). The following should be noted: improvisation, chance, moment of imprecision, interchangeability, indefiniteness, emptiness; reduction to pure motion, pure action, absolute motion, motoricity, *mouvement pur*. Arbitrary, blind movement is the guiding principle of the entire album, as emerges already from its title. That title applies insofar as the avant-garde was all along bent on movement, as conceived not only by the philosophy of history but also by sociology. Each one of its groups not only believed itself to be anticipating a phase of the historic process but also saw itself always as movement, motion. This movement, in both senses of the word, now proclaims itself an end in itself. The kinship with totalitarian movements lies close to hand, their center being precisely, as Hannah Arendt has shown, empty kinetic activity, which spews forth thor-

oughly arbitrary, indeed manifestly absurd, ideological demands and proceeds to implement them.[13] Kerouac's appeal,
"Strike as deep as you can strike!" is so utterly innocuous only
because it is directed at literature, and because literature, like
all arts, cannot be terrorized by the likes of him. Transposed
onto the plane of politics, it could serve as a device for any
fascist organization. The impotent avant-garde must content
itself with obliterating its own products. Quite consistently,
the Japanese painter Murakami contrives a large painted
paper screen destined for his work, which is "the piercing of
several holes in one instant"; "the work of Murakami made a
mighty noise as it was being pierced. Six holes were torn into
the strong eightfold paper screen. This was done with such
speed, in a single moment, that the cameramen [!] missed the
exact instant. When the six holes were there, he had an attack
of bloodlessness of the brain. 'I've been a new man ever since,'
he later murmured." [14]

All avant-garde groups incline toward the adoption of obscure doctrines of salvation. They are, characteristically, de-
fenseless against Zen Buddhism, which, within a few years,
spread rapidly among writers, painters, and musicians of this
cast. In its imported form, Zen Buddhism serves to confer
upon blind action an occult, quasi-religious consecration. Its
teachings are transmitted in *exempla,* the so-called *mondo.*
The punch line of the best-known *exemplum* consists in the
master's answering the metaphysical questions of a disciple
with a stick or a slap in the face. Murakami's "action" too
may be considered a Zen precept. It points to the latent acts
of violence in avant-garde "movements," which, to be sure,
are directed first against the "materials" with which they are
dealing: they blindly toss about paints, tones, or word frag-
ments rather than hurling hand grenades or Molotov cock-
tails.

The reverse side of this susceptibility to extremely irrational, supposedly mystical teachings is the no less extreme
faith in science that the avant-garde proudly sports. The indeterminacy of its "actions" always pretends to be exact. It
tries to convey this impression by means of a terminology for

which the most diverse disciplines have been ransacked: along with *vacuum* and *absolute motion,* there are catchwords like *constellation, material structure, correlogram, coordination, rotomodulation, microarticulation, phase-shift, autodetermination, transformation,* and so on and so forth. A laboratory smock enfolds the breast shot through with visionary spasms; and what the avant-garde produces, whether it be poems, novels, pictures, movies, constructions, or pieces of music, is and remains "experimental." 1805274

Experiment as an esthetic concept has long since become part of the vocabulary of the consciousness industry. Put in circulation by the avant-garde, used as an adjuration, worn threadbare and unelucidated, it haunts artistic conferences and cultural panels and reproduces itself through reviews and essays. The obligatory modifier is *bold,* but the choice of the ennobling epithet *courageous* is also permitted. The most modest reflection reveals that it is a case of plain bluff.

Experimentum means "that which has been experienced." In modern languages, the Latin word designates a scientific procedure for the verification of theories or hypotheses through methodical observation of natural phenomena. The process to be explained must be isolable. An experiment is meaningful only when the variables that appear are known and can be controlled. There is the additional requisite that every experiment must be susceptible of rechecking and must at every repetition yield the same unequivocal result. That is to say, an experiment can succeed or miscarry only with regard to a previously exactly defined goal. It presupposes reflection and contains an experience. It can in no way be an end in itself: its intrinsic worth equals zero. Let us also set down that a genuine experiment has nothing to do with boldness. It is a very simple and indispensable procedure for the investigation of laws. It requires, above all, patience, acuteness, circumspection, and diligence.

Pictures, poems, performances do not satisfy these requirements. The experiment is a procedure for bringing about scientific insights, not for bringing about art. (Of course, every publication can be considered an economic or sociological experiment. Under this heading, success and failure can be established quite accurately, and most publishers, art dealers, and theatrical managers do not hesitate to derive from that the theory and practice of their enterprises. To be sure, viewed from this angle, Karl May is every bit as experimental as Jack Kerouac. The difference between the two experiments lies in the result, that is, in the number of copies sold. That such experiments possess esthetic relevance may be doubted.) Experiment as bluff does, indeed, flirt with the scientific method and its demands, but has not the least intention of getting seriously involved with it.[15] It is unconditional "pure action"; intentions of any kind are not to be attributed to it. Method, possibility of proof, stringency have no share in it. The farther removed from any sort of experience they are, the more the experiments of the avant-garde are "experimental."

That proves that this concept is nonsensical and unusable. What has yet to be explained is what makes it so popular. That is not hard to say. A biologist who undertakes an experiment on a guinea pig cannot be held accountable for its behavior. He is answerable only for the irreproachable observance of the conditions of the experiment. The result is out of his hands; the experimenter is literally obligated to interfere as little as possible in the process he is observing. The moral immunity he enjoys is precisely what appeals to the avant-garde. Though it is by no means ready to adhere to the methodical demands to which the scientist submits, it does wish to avoid all responsibility, both for its activities and their results. It hopes to achieve this by referring to the "experimental" character of its work. The borrowings from science serve as an excuse. With the designation *experiment,* the avant-garde excuses its results, takes back, as it were, its "actions," and unloads all responsibility on the receiver. Every boldness suits the avant-garde perfectly so long as it itself remains safe. The concept of the experiment is to insure it against the risk of all esthetic production. It serves both as trademark and as camouflage.

What is under investigation here is the aporias of the avant-garde, its concept, its assumptions, and its postures. Such an analysis reveals the claims made in behalf of concrete poetry, the beat generation, tachism, and other present-day avant-garde groupings to be untenable, each and all. On the other hand, it can by no means serve the purpose of condemning the productions of such groups as a whole. It does not unmask doctrinaire fraud only to fall prey to it itself. Not a single work can be dismissed by pointing to the fact that its creator has joined up with such-and-such-a-guard, and even the silliest esthetic program does not *ipso facto* vitiate the potency of those who subscribe to it. The person who demolishes the terminological tricks and doctrinal screens with which today's avant-garde tries to shield itself does not thereby save himself the trouble of critically examining its products; he merely makes such a critical examination possible in the first place. Such examination must be insisted upon all the more determinedly the more advanced a work claims to be; and the more assiduously it appeals to a collective, the more it must affirm its individuality. Every popular movie deserves more leniency than an avant-garde that would simultaneously overpower critical judgment and timorously rid itself of the responsibility for its own works.

The aporias that have rent it and delivered it into the hands of charlatans have always been contained in the concept of the avant-garde. They were not first dragged in by hangers-on and stragglers. Already the first futurist manifesto of 1909, one of the earliest documents of an organized "movement," makes *"dynamisme perpétuel"* into an end in itself: "We live," Marinetti writes, "already in the absolute: we have created permanent and omnipresent speed. . . . We extol aggressive motion, feverish sleeplessness, marching on the double, the slap of the palm and the blow of the fist above all things. . . . There is no beauty but that of battle. . . . Only in war can the world recover its health." (The last sentence in the original: *"La guerre seule hygiène du monde."*)[16]

In futurism, the avant-garde organized itself for the first time as a doctrinaire clan, and already then it lauded blind action and open violence. That in 1924 the nucleus of the movement collectively rushed into the fascist camp is no accident. In formal matters, the futurists, exactly as did their descendants, advocated the removal of all "literary, grammatical and syntactic barriers." Even the disconnected slapping together of pseudo-mathematics and questionable mysticism can already be found among them. The painters of the movement declared in 1912 that they wished to "reinforce the emotions of the viewer according to a law of inner mathematics"; there is talk also of visions and ecstasies. In the futurist texts, mathematical formulas crop up alongside occult incantations and chaotic verbal debris.[17] The catechism of the avant-garde of 1961 contains hardly a sentence that was not formulated fifty years earlier by Marinetti and his circle. Be it mentioned in passing that the few significant authors of the movement left it shortly after the publication of the first manifestoes and that these manifestoes are the only texts futurism has left us.

An extensive survey of the countless avant-gardist collectives of the first half of the twentieth century is neither possible nor called for here. The role of most of them is overestimated. Literary and art historians, who, as is known, enumerate "currents" and "isms" with passionate fondness because that relieves them of concern with details, have accepted too many such group appellations as gospel truth instead of sticking to the particulars of the given works; indeed, they even, as it were, invented such movements a posteriori. Thus German expressionism became hypostatized into a collective manifestation which, in reality, never existed: many expressionists did not even live to hear the word *expressionism,* introduced into German literature in 1914 by Hermann Bahr. Heym and Trakl died before it came up; as late as 1955, Gottfried Benn declared that he did not know what it was supposed to mean;[18] Brecht and Kafka, Döblin and Jahnn never "joined a movement" that went by that name. Every historian can claim for himself the right to tie together manifestations and lump the manifold under one heading, but only on the condition of not confusing his auxiliary constructs with reality, whose representation they are meant to subserve.

In contrast to expressionism, surrealism was, from the outset, a collective enterprise that had at its disposal a well-developed doctrine. All previous and subsequent groupings seem, compared to it, impoverished, dilettantish, and inarticulate. Surrealism is the paradigm, the perfect model of all avant-gardist movements: once and for all it thought through to the end all their possibilities and limitations and unfurled all the aporias inherent in such movements.

"Only the word freedom can still fill me with enthusiasm. I consider it suited to keep the old human fanaticism upright for an indefinite length of time yet to come." With these words, André Breton, in the year 1924, opens the first surrealist manifesto.[19] The new doctrine crystallizes, as always, around its yearning for absolute freedom. The word *fanaticism* is already an indication that this freedom can be acquired only at the price of absolute discipline; within a few years, the surrealist guard spins itself into a cocoon of regulations. The tighter the bond to the collective, the blinder the "pure action": "The simplest surrealist deed consists," we read in Breton, "in walking out into the street with guns in the hand and shooting as long as possible blindly into the crowd." A few years were yet to pass before this maxim was realized in Germany. In any case, even before World War II broke out, Salvador Dali reached the conclusion that "Hitler is the greatest surrealist." [20]

Long before the coming to power of this surrealist, inner aporias had split open the movement. Its sociology would deserve more detailed consideration. At the end of the twenties, the intrigues, declarations of apostasy, bickerings, and "purges" within the group reached their high point. Its development into a narrow-minded sect strikes one as both ridiculous and tragic; yet it cannot be stemmed by the energy and self-sacrifice of the members because it follows of necessity from the presuppositions of the movement.[21] Its commander-in-chief assumes more and more the features of a revolutionary pope; he sees himself compelled solemnly to excommunicate his companions-in-arms one after another. Occasionally this turns into show trials that, in retrospect, seem like bloodless parodies of the later Stalinist purges. At the outbreak of World War II, the surrealist movement lost all its best brains without exception: Artaud, Desnos, Soupault, Duchamp, Aragon, Éluard, Char, Queneau, Leiris, and many others turned their backs on it. Since then, the group ekes out a shadowy existence.

The party-line surrealist literature is faded and forgotten; the above-named authors have, with the exception of Breton, produced nothing worth mentioning while submitting to the group's discipline. Surrealism was destined to have an enormous effect, but it became productive only in those who freed themselves from its doctrine.[22]

We see no reason for gloating over its foundering. Every backward glance at an avant-garde whose future is known has an easy time of it. Everyone today participates in the historical experiences of surrealism. No one has the right to encounter it with condescension or to take pleasure in its plight; it is, however, our duty to draw conclusions from its downfall. The law of increasing reflection is inexorable. Whoever tries to dodge it ends up offered for sale at a discount by the consciousness industry. Every avant-garde of today spells repetition, deception, or self-deception. The movement as a doctrinairely conceived collective, as invented fifty or thirty years ago for the purpose of shattering the resistance of a compact society, did not survive the historic conditions that elicited it. Conspiring in the name of the arts is only possible where they are being suppressed. An avant-garde that suffers itself to be furthered by the state has forfeited its rights.

The historic avant-garde perished by its aporias. It was questionable, but it was not craven. Never did it try to play it safe with the excuse that what it was doing was nothing more than an "experiment"; it never cloaked itself in science in order to be absolved of its results. That distinguishes it from the company of limited responsibility that is its successor; therein lies its greatness. In 1942, when, except for him, nobody believed in surrealism any more, Breton raised his voice against "all those who do not know that there is no great departure in art that does not take place in mortal peril, that the road to be taken quite obviously is not protected by a breastwork, and that every artist must set out all alone on the quest for the Golden Fleece."

This is no plea for a "middle way" and no cue for an about-face. The path of the modern arts is not reversible. Let others harbor hopes for the end of modernity, for conversions and "re-integrations." What is to be chalked up against today's avant-garde is not that it has gone too far but that it keeps the back doors open for itself, that it seeks support in doctrines and collectives, and that it does not become aware of its own aporias, long since disposed of by history. It deals in a future that does not belong to it. Its movement is regression. The avant-garde has become its opposite: anachronism. That inconspicuous, limitless risk, by which the artists' future lives—it cannot sustain it.

Translated by John Simon.

The world language of modern poetry

1. MODERNITY'S PAST

Modern poetry is one hundred years old. It is part of history. But how far back does the concept of modernity extend? In the sense of being of recent origin, modernity itself is by no means modern. It is a late Latin word that came into use at the turn of the fifth century, and to trace its course through the European languages is a topic for dissertations. Ever since the term "modernity" was first used, it has caused agitation and confusion; a certain arbitrariness is inseparable from it. Only by mutual agreement to treat each case separately can modernity be given a precise meaning. Thus, in what follows, modern poetry is taken to mean poetry since Whitman and Baudelaire, Rimbaud and Mallarmé. *Leaves of Grass* appeared in 1855, *Les Fleurs du Mal* in 1857. Modernity, unambiguous and radiant, was present in the work of those few "individual profound natures" who thrust up, "like dammed-up springs," in the second half of the last century and "traded in arcana" (Brentano). It was Rimbaud who raised modernity to an unequivocal demand: *"Il faut être absolument moderne!"*

But scarcely had modern poetry been discovered than it discovered within itself the demand for a theory. This demand was offset by another: the refusal of modern poetry to allow itself to be shackled by theory. The concept of modernity has exhausted itself in movements and countermovements, manifestoes and countermanifestoes. Its energy is spent. Today it serves the dull purposes of propaganda on behalf of the existing order, against which it once promised to be an explosive and liberating force. It has found its way like a ghost into the vocabulary of the world of consumer goods. Modernity has become the demand for nothing-but-modern, is put at the mercy of journalistic consent, is a fungible impetus in industrial production.

2. TRADITIONALISM, AVANT-GARDE

Thus modern poetry today finds itself exposed to attack from two sides. Its old opponents scent an advantage. They play with the notion of the end of the modern era, of the loss of the center, which they hope to find again at once, of the conquest of nihilism, for which they hold unruly poetry responsible, and of the golden postrevolutionary age into which they would like to transplant us. They think they can dispose of what is modern by declaring it out-of-date. In the same breath in which they call Mayakovsky irrelevant, these strange guardians of Western heritage play off Virgil and Dante against him. In the name of tradition they attack what is modern without grasping the fact that it too has long been part of tradition. But modern poetry also has its blind partisans whose applause is no less harmful than reactionary opposition. Those who deny the historic distance separating us from Benn's *Morgue* and Schwitters' *Blume Anna,* who are intent on making an unmediated connection to the past and pretend that something is new which has spared itself the trouble of taking the few necessary steps in time, are the ones who loudly claim membership in the avant-garde. The stimulus of avant-garde as an idea has long since diminished; like the idea of modernity, it has grown barren and slaggy in proportion as the aporia, inherent in it from the beginning, have developed historically. To count himself among the vanguard, a man must see the arts as marching columns which have fallen into line behind him. The deadliness of this view of the advance of the productive forces was recognized by Baudelaire when that conception was still in its infancy: "This habit of putting one's trust in military metaphors is characteristic not of unyielding minds but of minds that prefer discipline, in other words conformity, of minds in fetters, provincial minds that can think only collectively." [1] Faced by modernity, traditionalism today turns into a hatred of history, and the avant-garde into commercialized artiness.

3. POETRY AS A PROCESS

Opponents and followers alike threaten to turn modern poetry into a phantom. The only way to oppose this is to show and comprehend it as an inevitable element in our tradition, the latest and most powerful. [2] What matters is to protect it as much from mere admiration as from oblivion and imitation. Its readers must measure themselves against it and indeed subject it, *ad liminem,* to productive annihilation—an act that always causes the old (even the old among the modern) to rise, phoenix-like, anew. Properly understood, this should be the task of historical criticism, which should not mummify the past but expose it to the grasp of those who have come subsequently. The tradition of modernity is challenge, not consecration.

This is evident, but not self-evident; for scholarship when applied to art, and hence to poetry, tends all too readily to regard its subject as an arsenal, an ensemble of individual works, and is thus untrue to its historic calling. Poetry is a process, a process moreover which no museum, not even an imaginary one, can arrest. To try to arrest it is to reify the poetic act into a fetish, with the result that the work is seen as a timeless, transportable art treasure, in which what is allegedly unperishable is embodied as a gilt-edged security. Such a viewpoint has a certain validity in that an individual work can withstand the corroding forces of history over long periods, but it forgets that the process not only injures and devours the works it calls to life, branding them with the scars of fame and oblivion; the process also supports them, keeps them alive and gives them new strength. The motives of ownership and investment, which hoard works of art as capital and stock for eternity, are always unjust to what they preserve. Scholarship, inasmuch as it partakes of those motives, is in the same position; even those of its basic notions which give evidence of real insight into art as a process—epochs and trends, schools and movements—can grow rigid and manipulable if scholarship's awareness of their tenuousness disappears.

Many of the ideas on which literary scholarship depends to classify the multifariousness of modern poetry have this sort of devitalizing and mummifying effect. They were invented by the poets themselves and not always for the best reasons: for reasons of tactics or convenience, for example, or even by mistake. The list of "movements," from futurism to tremendism, from vorticism to concrete poetry, comprises a good two dozen names. Even today many of these are still accepted at their face value in seminars and literary histories, yet a certain mistrust of them is advisable. The help these labels provide for diagnosis is small. They blur one's view of the individual work by making it subject to a doctrine; they obstruct one's view of the whole by diverting one's attention to rival groups, most of which in any case are confined within their own linguistic orbits.

4. DESTRUCTION OF, AND RECOURSE TO, THE PAST; NEGATION OF NEGATION

Whether the motive is good or bad, statements to the effect that modern poetry has broken with the works of the past and discarded them, has even superseded or disposed of them, demolished or been victorious over them, are highly questionable. Such hasty victory is always suspect; the victor whose victory has cost him nothing is apt to be the first to parade it. The truth is that modern poetry has always had a better knowledge than its conservative opponents of what preceded it. *Il faut être absolument moderne* has meant repudiation of the status quo, destruction of all inheritance, radical negation of literary history in the mutilated form practiced in academies of learning. It has meant revolt, but it has also meant intensive study of the masters, acceptance of the challenge of their works, reabsorption of the past in the act of writing. What cannot be preserved in this way cannot be saved. Literature alone can write literary history, not only its own but that of any age. Modern poetry has transformed in this way, for our eyes, everything that preceded it right back to poetry's beginnings. It is to our "heritage" that we owe the destruction of what these poets found. It would be instructive to compile a list of their masters; this would contain everything of the past that has power to move us. Apollinaire and Breton studied Novalis and Brentano. Ezra Pound's canon, expounded in numerous theoretical writings, extends from the classic lyric poetry of China to the verses of the troubadours, from the poetry of Sappho to the prose of Flaubert. Brecht's work is stamped by his encounter with the works of Lucretius and Horace, Villon, Luther's translation of the Psalms, and the Nō plays of Japan. The great Spanish poets of our century have rediscovered, indeed they have unfettered, the old ballads of Lope de Vega, Quevedo and Góngora. Modern poetry is permeated by echoes of Catullus, images derived from Indian and Bantu poetry, reminiscences of the haiku of Japan, the chorus of Greek tragedy, the verses of the Vedas and the metaphysical poets, the arts of the fairy tale and the madrigal. This diversity is a special feature of our century.

The unfolding of historic consciousness, supported by the techniques of reproduction, has made such headway that we have the whole range of artistic material, however distant it may be in space or time, within effortless reach. To the poet this wealth, and the ease with which he can avail himself of it, is both an opportunity and a danger. It has been rightly observed that with modernity the hour of the *poeta doctus* has struck. Whether it parades or hides its knowledge, it is certain that in times like these every important poetic work must refract and absorb an enormous irradiation from tradition.

Destruction of, and recourse to, the past is a side of the process of modern poetry which has been insufficiently examined so far. Only what appears in its entirety within our field of vision can be described. Until now the prerequisites for such a description have been lacking. There is an immense amount of translation to be done before we can survey the phenomenon.

A start has been made. The war and its aftermath, and in Germany the relapse into barbarism long before that, delayed it for decades. However, the keener our eye as we look back over this poetry, the clearer it becomes that destruction, the law by which it made its way, has been transformed into construction. Disintegration, subversion, nihilism, capriciousness, vandalism—or whatever slurs reactionary indignation has cast on the motivating forces of modern poetry—have created and consolidated a new linguistic situation. What is remarkable is how little attention has been paid to this constructive feature, which the process has manifested from its inception; it is as if Marinetti's and Breton's cries of destruction were still ringing in our ears today. The silly question about the positive contribution of modern poetry has not been silenced either, although the code of modern poetry is now so firmly established that even lesser minds seem capable of acquiring it, thus effecting an epigonous modern tradition. This is not surprising. He who continues to shake his head and question modern poetry about its positive contribution fails to see the obvious fact that to act "negatively" is poetically impossible; the reverse side of all poetic destruction is the construction of new poetry.

True, this will not respond to traditional treatment, and the most we can hope for is to present it descriptively; the days of the rule book are gone—forever. Preliminary studies, descriptive approaches to a theory of modern poetry, have been made, but nothing more. Montage and ambiguity, dissolution and change in the function of rhyme, dissonance and absurdity, a dialectic of proliferation and reduction, estrangement and mathematization, long-line technique, irregular rhythms, freedom of stress and phrasing, contrasting syntactical constructions, the use of allusion and obscurity, discovery of new metaphoric techniques, experiments with new syntactical procedures—these are only some of the terms and categories that have been summoned to the aid of a theoretical understanding of modern poetry. To what extent they are apposite and serviceable, only reference to the texts themselves can tell. We still await an authoritative and critical exposition that will reveal the inner connection between these various manifestations.

5. ANTECEDENTS

Like its poetics, the history of modern poetry still has to be written. It will not be possible to confine it to the twentieth century, for the silent catastrophes in a language do not occur from one day to the next, or even from one generation to the next. They have a long gestation period, and we have to go back to the romantics to find the first traces of the ferment that distinguishes the language of poetry during the last hundred years. One could say, though with some exaggeration, that the first theoretic precipitation of modern poetry occurred before it came into existence, in the work of Novalis. The genesis of historicism, that revolution in consciousness analyzed by Friedrich Meinecke, occurred at the same time, and is the prerequisite and historico-intellectual correlative of that self-conscious process by which the poetic language of modernity develops. The political equivalent to these historico-literary and historico-intellectual *terminis a quibus* is the great French Revolution. However inadequately these may have been evaluated and secured, there is an urgent need to insist on their validity vis-à-vis every approach that seeks to trace modern poetry back to ever-recurring "structures," thereby making it disappear by claiming that it had always existed. The history of poetry, like all history, is irreversible. It does not repeat itself. Only an a-historical approach, limiting itself to a noncommittal examination of phenomenological patterns, can disregard this—without, of course, being innocent of wishing to draw the teeth from ever-disturbing modernity so as to domesticate it.

The process of modern poetry becomes productive in the middle of the nineteenth century. Although the list of chief protagonists was named at the outset, it is provisional and admits of additions and corrections. Gérard de Nerval and Edgar Allen Poe, Emily Dickinson and the Comte de Lautréamont, Gerard Manley Hopkins and Jules Laforgue, Alexander Block and William Butler Yeats might well appear in it, but this catalogue virtually exhausts the significant names. Until the first decade of the twentieth century, modern poetry was the concern of only a very few exceptional intellects, of those "individual profound natures" whose appearance Brentano predicted. While one can establish individual affinities between them, there can be no question of their works forming a whole. Each had to rely on himself in a hostile age and pay for the title "contemporary" which accrued to him later, with isolation and disdain. These poets spoke to the future, to the echoless halls of history.

6. CONTEXT

With the beginning of the twentieth century the process of modern poetry entered a new phase. There is really no doubt when this started; its threshold was the year 1910. At that time a chain of literary explosions shook the reading public in all the advanced countries. The first volume of Ezra Pound's poems appeared in 1908, followed a year later by the first verses of William Carlos Williams; 1909 also saw, together with the futurist manifesto, the publication of St.-John Perse's *Images à Crusoé*. In 1910 expressionism made its appearance in Germany with *Der Sturm* and *Die Aktion,* Chlebnikov's first poems were printed in Russia, and those of Kavafis in Alexandria. Guillaume Apollinaire, Gottfried Benn, Max Jacob and Vladimir Mayakovsky followed in 1912, and Guiseppe Ungaretti and Boris Pasternak a year later. These dates are easily interchangeable with many others of equal significance. They indicate that henceforth modern poetry was no longer a matter of individual writers and works which, like foundlings, were strangers in their day; it had become contemporary. Simultaneously, in the most diverse parts of the Western world, and shortly afterwards in the Eastern, there appeared publications, at first sporadically and often quite independently of one another, which soon began to form an international context.

The change was qualitative and not comparable to previous historic ruptures. In the few decades that have passed since the stormy year of 1910, modern poetry has established its dominance throughout the world. Its poets have established a rapport among themselves that has lifted the national barriers of poetry as never before and given the concept of world literature a lustre inconceivable in other ages. In many cases this rapport has a biographical basis. Among the leaders of modern poetry have been several who were very quick to gain an overview of their context and who, as guides and translators, critics and essayists, set out to make it explicit and manifest. If literary scholarship were less imprisoned by national languages, here would be an ideal terrain for research; and the search for influences and direct reciprocal effects may occasionally produce a subaltern element. However, the chief feature of this international rapport has been its independence from such influences. Between Santiago de Chile and Helsinki, Prague and Madrid, New York and Leningrad, one keeps finding absolutely astonishing coincidences, but they are not traceable to any mutual dependence. The fact that this or that poet has read the others does not explain the phenomenon. Quite the opposite is the case. In the most disparate areas of the world, writers who have never heard of each other are simultaneously and independently encountering the same problems and finding the same solutions. The era of international literary exhibitions and biennials, at which each country was represented by its own pavilion, is over. Poetry no longer is nationalistic. The great masters of modern poetry, from Chile to Japan, have more in common than do all those who parade their national origin.

This supranational trait finds exemplary expression in the careers of a number of writers. In 1880 a certain Guillaume-

Albert-Vladimir-Apollinaire Kostrovitsky was born in Rome; the register of births contains an entry under the name Guillaume-Albert Dulcigni. The child's mother, born in Helsinki, came of a Polish-Russian family; the father was a Sicilian named Francesco Constantino Camillo Flugi d'Aspermont. Throughout his life Guillaume Apollinaire, as he later called himself, wrote in French, like the Lithuanian Oscar Wenceslas de Lubicz Milosz, the Chilean Vicente Huidobro (who also wrote in Spanish), the black poet Aimé Césaire from Basse-Pointe, Martinique, and the Alsatian Jean Arp, who signs his German poetry Hans Arp. The Peruvian Vallejo died in Paris, the Turk Hikmet lives in Moscow as a Russian citizen, and the American Pound lived in Italy. Supervielle, who was born in Uruguay, was a citizen of both hemispheres. The Chilean Neruda wrote his poems in Djakarta, Mexico, Madrid, Paris, Buenos Aires, and Moscow. The Greek Kavafis was born in Constantinople, educated in England, and spent his life in Egypt. The list can be continued almost indefinitely. A person setting out to claim poets such as these for any one country would find himself in no small dilemma. Today it is less possible than ever to demand of poetry a passport. Such biographical details deserve to be recorded because their significance is more than just superficial and they serve to show how little can be achieved, in the face of modern poetry, by the concept of autonomous national literatures.

7. DOUBT AND HYPOTHESIS

What are we discussing? Modern poetry. However, are we using the expression seriously? Literary scholarship has long been accused of replacing subjects by names and employing these names, glibly and superficially, because it is convenient. Does anyone know, for instance, precisely what the "Renaissance" is or was? Has anyone ever met "baroque man"? These are awkward questions, and Ernst Robert Curtius is the one who has asked them most trenchantly.[3] Shall we find in the end that "modern poetry" is merely a terminological sham?

Or, to put it differently, what guarantees the unity of the phenomenon, apart from a few dates?

It is not the first time that poetry has crossed the barriers of country and language. One could even say with some justification that the idea of a world literature is older than that of a national literature; Greek and Latin poetry were acknowledged throughout the whole "civilized world," *urbi et orbi,* and by no means only in their mother countries. This is even truer of medieval Latin poetry, indeed of the whole lyric and epic production of the Middle Ages, and no less of the "baroque" or "mannerist" poetry of the seventeenth century. Compared to all this the idea of an autarchically conceived national literature, like the idea of nationhood itself, is recent. But what earlier ages regarded as *orbis* was always restricted to their own limited horizon: the world meant the world between Miletus and Marsilia, and later between London and Naples—beyond it lived savages. Even Goethe's postulate of a world literature was a European affair, idealistic and limited, and far removed from planetary reality. Only in the twentieth century has "world" become the prefix to every productive and destructive possibility: world war, world economy, world literature—in earnest this time, in deadly earnest, and as a condition of survival. With this the historic process has entered a radically new phase, of which we can survey scarcely more than its beginning, but of which we can say that it no longer permits any smug comparison with what preceded it. The conservative self-delusion that everything has already existed is politically perilous—look at Rome or Weimar; critics and scholars, too, can no longer be satisfied with the former scope of their activities, on pain of jeopardizing the validity of their output. *Historia fecit saltus*—criticism must take cognizance of history's leap from national to world history.

Modern poetry owes its unity not only to its nearly simultaneous origins in many countries, to the fact that horizons throughout the world have widened, to the converging social conditions which, with advancing development, it finds everywhere (we shall return to these); but also a common awareness is reflected in the works themselves. Increasingly they invite comparison after comparison, answer each other often without knowledge of one another, travel like pollen into the unknown, over every continent, and propagate in the furthest corners. This conversation, this exchange of voices and echoes, is becoming more and more obvious, and one has only to place side by side metaphors, cadences, techniques, and themes from a dozen languages to become aware of this. In other words, the process of modern poetry is leading to the formation of a world language of poetry. At present this remains a hypothesis verifiable only by reference to hundreds of examples, theoretically plausible but incapable of proof. On the other hand it is possible, with the aid of a few words, to protect this hypothesis from misunderstandings which could destroy its usefulness.

8. PROVINCIALISM, UNIVERSALITY

Wherever one goes today the word "provincialism" is bandied about, either in the form of criticism or as self-reproach. Never has the fear of being provincial been more widespread than it is now. And the fear is unfounded, because it presupposes the existence of readily accepted centers of culture whose role as arbiter in all intellectual questions is uncontested. In the past this role has fallen to the lot of two or three European capitals. It has now been played out, or at any rate leaves them no more than clearing centers. To speak of the provinces and mean the hinterland may have been possible in the Germany of the twenties, because of the splendor of Berlin; today not even London or Paris any longer has the last word in matters of critical opinion. The old habit of speaking of the capital on one hand and the provinces on the other had significance in our own country during the era of nationalism; in other parts of the world it was a sublimation of imperialistic trends of thought. To divorce the provinces from the capital is no longer reconcilable with our historical situation, in which even the powerful agglomerative forces of political ideologies have become inadequate to canonize a new Rome, and in which no "bloc" can any longer be certain of its monolithic structure. The word "provincialism" thus acquires a new meaning. Either the provinces comprise everything, because there is no longer a center of the world, or else the reverse is true, because essentially the world's *omphalos* can be presumed to be everywhere. Here literature is ahead of politics. The literary capital of the world could as well be Dublin as Alexandria; it is situated in Svendborg or Meudon, in Rutherford or Merano. An island off the Pacific coast of South America, a dacha in the Russian forest, a log cabin beside a Canadian lake are no less centrally situated than are the improbable London, Paris, or Lisbon dwellings to which writers like Eliot, Beckett, or Pessoa have withdrawn. The arrogance of the capitals has vanished along with the pejorative sense of the word "provinces." Its opposite is no longer Paris but universality, its reverse and its complement. The special quality, the dignity, of what is provincial is released from its reactionary inhibitions, from the pigheaded narrowness of the local museum, and assumes its rights; far from disappearing in the universality of the world language of poetry, it constitutes its vitality, just as the written language feeds off the spoken word of dialect. For the *lingua franca* of modern poetry is not to be thought of as vapid monotony, as a lyrical esperanto. It speaks in many tongues. It does not mean standardization, or the lowest common denominator, but the reverse. It frees poetry from the narrowness inherent in all national literature, but not in order to tear it from its provincial soil and transplant it in the abstract. It cuts right across the old languages. As a concept it is valid in the same way as the language of the Bible, or technical language, is valid. It differs from this last because it does more than serve a useful purpose, because it not only owes its existence to the national languages but revivifies them and unobtrusively changes them. Unlike the language of the Bible, it does not derive from one but from many sources; and it expounds no doctrine, except perhaps the one that it is no longer possible for any nation to sever its destiny from that of the others.

9. QUALIFICATION

What we have been saying does not hold true everywhere without qualification—not yet. Large areas of the world still take no part in the dialogue of modern poetry. But we should be ill-advised to deduce from this that world literature and world poetry were no more than a utopian dream or, as in the old days, a European phenomenon. The Asian and African countries certainly take too little part; but the absence of a Western monopoly is not only demonstrable, it has been demonstrated. A collection such as *Schwarzer Orpheus*[4] is sufficient proof of this; it shows that the black peoples can also speak the language of poetry in their own right, not merely as a result of colonial imitation, and that they can contribute new material to the common language. More striking still is the example of Japan, where despite the radically different tradition and the radically different structure of thought and language, a modern poetry has come into being in the last fifty years which need fear no comparison and which has undoubtedly won a place in the international context.[5] Moreover, despite its origin, Japanese poetry is nearer to our own, and also to that of America, Italy, and Scandinavia, for example, than is the poetry written in some European countries, such as Bulgaria or—until a few years ago—Finland.

The explanation for this can be found in the lack of true contemporaneity in some so-called contemporary production. Although the whole world writes the same date, it lives in different historical phases. If we examine the temporal and spatial development of the world language of poetry, we quickly notice that it coincides with the development of the productive forces of society. A highly developed technical civilization, with its inherent opportunities and drawbacks, is a prerequisite of its existence. In purely agricultural countries, with preindustrial standards, modern poetry does not appear until these standards are called into question; this is the reason for "cultural lags," including those in the language of poetry. The case of Japan is a perfect example of this interconnection, suggesting to us that in the foreseeable future, as soon as the requisite social conditions are fulfilled and the time lag made up, the process of modern poetry will also reach those lacuna in Asia and Africa which still remain untouched by it.

10. TECHNOLOGY, "ANTICOMMODITY"

However, the close interconnection between industrial methods of production and modern poetry can be demonstrated even more simply. The poets themselves express it clearly enough in their writings on poetry. It is over a hundred years since Edgar Allen Poe in his essay "The Philosophy of Composition" first described poets as technologists. His ideas had far-reaching influence, because they had discovered a fact that was crucial for modern poetry's understanding of itself. Valéry says of Baudelaire: "For him the demon of precision, the analytical genius . . . in short, the literary engineer, made his appearance in Edgar Poe." Mallarmé, too, was deeply affected by Poe's insight and understanding. It is remarkable how directly esoteric writers—the pure artists in their approach to poetry—have made reference to the industrial revolution, a socially determined environment. What they say scarcely differs from what the rabidly tendentious political poet Vladimir Mayakovsky says in his pamphlet *How One Makes Verses,* where he analyzes poetic output by making methodical use of industrial terminology, distinguishing between poetic raw materials, semifinished and finished products.[6] Thus we find the technological character of the modern approach to poetry expressed more precisely in the writings of its founders than in the technical and scientific expressions which have become familiar and dull in literary criticism (montage, word laboratory, experiment, constellation, structural element).

However, one should not jump to conclusions in trying to understand the connection between poetry and technical civilization; it is not without one hitch or another. Conventional Marxism, which says "superstructure" when it means unmediated economic determination, runs afoul of modern poetry, which keeps abreast of prevailing methods of production, but as one keeps abreast of an enemy. The statement that a poem is not a commodity is no mere idealistic phrase. From the outset modern poetry has aimed at freeing the poem from the law of the market place. The poem is the anticommodity par excellence; this was and is the social significance of all the theories about *poésie pure.* In making this challenge modern poetry is defending poetry as a whole, and it maintains its position against every pressure that tries to force it into the ideological market place. In any case, to contrast ivory tower and agit prop renders poetry no useful service; it is a clash of words as pointless as the exertions of two mice chasing each other in the treadmill of a cage. The anticommodity, which resists manipulation on "pure" grounds, becomes Mayakovsky's most completely engaged "finished product." And the mere fact that it is poetry transforms the trapeze acts of Arp or Éluard into *poésie engagée:* conflict, not agreement, with what exists.

11. THE UNINTELLIGIBLE, THE SELF-EVIDENT

This conflict has always elicited the reproach that modern poetry is "unintelligible," a remarkable characteristic of the reproach being that it is never made specifically, to a particular piece of writing, but is always levelled at modern poetry as a whole. This arouses the suspicion that the reproach is based not on genuine reading experience but on dislike. If this were not so, word would surely have leaked out that intelligibility and unintelligibility mean something quite different according to whether one refers to a poem by Brecht, Apollinaire, or Pound. Each of these writers presents his readers with different problems. To say that they are *all* unintelligible means something else again: it proclaims and simultaneously conceals the fact that in the past poetry, like culture in general, has always been for the few, the happy few.

To reproach the poets with being unintelligible is to make them the scapegoats for our alienation, as though it were solely up to them to put an end to it overnight. True, we now have at our disposal the technical means to make culture available to all, but the industry that handles these means reproduces the social conflicts that prevent the realization of this; in fact, it aggravates these conflicts by adding intellectual to material exploitation, and its centrifugal effect on the productive forces separates them so completely as to confront poetry with the choice of renouncing either itself or its public. The result is on the one hand an increasingly high-bred poetry for a public converging on zero, and on the other, sharply distinguished from it, the wholesale and increasingly primitive supply of poetic surrogates, whether in the commercialized forms of best-seller, digest, film, and television, or in the state-promoted form of political propaganda.

However trite it sounds, it is still worth our while to reflect briefly on the reproach of unintelligibility levelled at modern poetry. Inasmuch as it reminds us of the obscurity common to all poems, it contains an element of truth. Pindar and Goethe are also obscure, but their "unintelligibility" has been forgotten, suppressed, rendered harmless. *Au fond* the classics are no less intolerable than the moderns; their poetry too is conflict. But this intolerable fact is not to be admitted; and to disguise it, render it harmless, and make it acceptable, society has created special institutions, whose mills, of course, grind slowly. Modern poetry has not yet passed through them; hence the hostility which it still encounters. The unintelligibility for which it is reviled is, in the last analysis, the "self-evident" of which all great works speak and which remains forgotten, because society will neither tolerate nor admit it.

Because modern poetry reminds us of what is self-evident but has been withheld from us, it has been abused and persecuted whenever naked force has made its appearance in history. The measures dictatorships adopt to oppose it are proof of its power. Its small, limited dissemination, statistically speaking, bears no relation, oddly enough, to its unforeseeable and incalculable influence. Poetry is a trace element. Its mere existence calls into question the status quo, which is the reason why force cannot come to terms with it and all totalitarian regimes find it intolerable. The list of banned and burned books is endless; modern poetry occupies a place of honor in it. The careers of many of its best writers have been branded by fascist and Stalinist terror; the number of those exiled and murdered is nearly uncountable: died in exile, killed in the civil war, driven to suicide, murdered in a concentration camp, perished in jail, tortured and shot in Germany, Spain, and Russia—that has been the end for many of the poets of our century. They are witness to the fact that modern poetry is not possible without freedom, that if it does not embody a portion of freedom it ceases to exist.

12. FORMALISM

What a peculiar conflict! Afflicted on the one hand by fearful persecutions, suppressed, always under the threat of force, this poetry has announced from the beginning, as a basic tenet: "Exclude reality, it is vulgar" (Mallarmé); "The poet has no subject" (Reverdy); "Lyric poetry has no subject other than the poet himself" (Benn). Theorists of modern poetry are tireless in ringing changes on the theme: modern poetry needs only to speak of nothing in order to be pure form. This thesis of the emptiness of the modern poem finds its historic justification in modern poetry's quarrel with the stupid question "What does the poet have to say to us?," with attitudes current in the nineteenth century and still the fashion from Leipzig to Peking. Then as now, this attitude has demanded the comprehensible, the uncritically conformist, the positive, the socially acceptable—demands we know only too well; they can be heard whenever a state of emergency is about to be proclaimed for all of art. On this our Western guardians of the Holy Grail, members of the Nazi *Reichsschrifttumskammer,* and Communist cultural officials easily agree. Formalism is a crime to them because it expresses things that should be camouflaged: lack of freedom and alienation. But this is no reason for us to take seriously a false alternative which the enemies of poetry would like to dictate to us. The dispute between form and content, like that between *poésie pure* and *poésie engagée,* is based on a pseudo-problem. But those who become entangled in it have their reasons. The spokesmen for the reactionary approach would be happiest if they could put formalism behind bars; those of the deadbeat avant-garde cling to it as an ideology by whose means they can hide the fact that they have nothing to say.[7] It can do no harm to remind ourselves of a truth that is in danger of being forgotten because it is simple and not open to doubt: modern poetry, like all poetry, speaks of something, of matters which concern us.

13. THE FUTURE OF MODERN POETRY

In some countries, especially in those where it first developed, there have been signs of exhaustion in the language of modern poetry since the end of World War II. Poetry is no less liable to age than any other historical phenomenon. Fascism and war, the world's disintegration into hostile blocs, the elimination of alternatives, and the mobilization for destruction have all had a profoundly disturbing effect on the rapport between the poets. Auschwitz and Hiroshima were also epoch-making for poetry. Only those for whom the great historic rifts provide an alibi for history can suppose them to have no harmful effect on poetry. Inwardness is unteachable, it recognizes no epochs. Modern poetry, on the other hand, has had an overexposure to historic experience; it cannot help itself. The consciousness by which it is maintained is itself historic experience and cannot escape the law of progressive reflection.

Many of its great masters are dead. Other, younger poets are satisfied with mere continuation, as though modern poetry knew no differences and distinctions, as though it were a state and not a process, as though it could be turned into a conventional game. Its more distinguished representatives,

however, began long ago to analyze it. Poetry today presupposes not only knowledge but criticism of modern poetry;
indeed, production and criticism are no longer separable.

Nothing is lost by such reminders, such warnings. The position of those who saddle modernity with its past, like a
mortgage, as if everything great had already been done and
the only possibility left were to copy, exploit, imitate, or
capitulate, is not clever but contemptible. "Everything has
been done already" is the maxim of cowardice, of impotence.
Poetry is always incomplete, a torso whose missing limbs lie
in the future. It lacks tasks and opportunities no more than
it lacks tradition; whether it has sufficient strength to accept
these challenges is not for the critic to say. His office is to determine the present position, not to make predictions and
cast horoscopes. The future of modern poetry lies in the hands
of the unknown men who will write it.

Translated by Michael Roloff.

Poetry
and politics

The state decides what poets may or may not write—
that is a nightmare as old as the Occident. Decency and
good behavior must be observed. The gods are always
good. Statesmen and officials may not be disparaged in public.
Praise be to heroes, no matter what. The crimes of our rulers
are not fit subjects for poetry but for committee meetings behind closed doors. Protect our youth! Therefore, no portrayal
of unbridled passion unless it is authorized by the state. Irony
is forbidden. There must be no effeminacy. Poets, being born
liars, are to be assigned to the public-relations detail. The
control commission not only assigns topics, it also decrees
what forms are admissible and what tone of voice is desired.
The demand is for harmony at all costs; this means "good
language and good harmony and grace and good rhythm,"
in a word, affirmation. Nuisances will be exiled or eliminated, their works banned, censored, and mutilated.

These familiar maxims, formulated in a small Balkan state
more than two thousand years ago, can be found at the root
of all European discussion on poetry and politics.[1] They have
since spread across the entire world. Dully, monotonously,
brutally, they clang through history with the terrible regu-
larity of a steam hammer. They do not question what poetry
is, but treat it simply as an instrument to influence those held
in subjection, as something to be used at will in the interests
of authority. Hence the tenacious life of these maxims, for
they are tools of power—the selfsame thing into which they
are trying to turn poetry. For this reason they are passed from
hand to hand through history, like bludgeons, fungible, easily
detachable from the philosophy from which they were hewn.
Not only do they serve Platonism as cudgels against Aeschylus

and Homer, they serve every political administration. Christianity, feudalism, absolute monarchy, capitalism, fascism, and communism have all adapted Plato's doctrine; even in our own day and in the freest countries not a month goes by in which poetry is not put on trial, according to the Platonic prescription, for blasphemy, licentiousness, or as a danger to the state. In fact, this trial has lasted since Plato's day, and the variety of works incriminated proves that the trial was initiated not against this or that individual poem but against poetry as a whole. It continues to drag on from case to case, from court to court, and there is no sign that it is approaching its end. The same old speeches are exchanged between prosecution and defense, and the trial is still heard before incompetent tribunals and commissions. Self-defense prompts us to intervene in these proceedings, as a sad necessity. It is utterly tedious to refute for the thousandth time the Platonic theses which have long since fallen into decay and sunk to the level of third-rate editorials. Poetry and politics always has been and still is, especially in Germany, a disagreeable and sometimes bloody theme, clouded by resentment and servility, suspicion and bad conscience.

This gives us even less excuse to leave the matter where it is. Indeed, the time seems to have come when we can filter the poisoned ideas and guide the old questions into new channels. Self-defense is not enough. Refuting the bailiffs with their writs still does not explain the relationship between poetry and politics. It may be more to the point to question not only poetry's prosecutors and defenders but poetry itself, which is likely to be more articulate than either. The more obscure the theme, the more transparent should be the methods of investigation. For the moment, therefore, let us content ourselves with what is simplest by looking at the surface of the matter and discussing the most obvious example: the political poem. We must first seek guidance where poetry does not immediately reject the Platonic and all subsequent simplifications, where it manifests its political nature.

In its beginnings poetry, no less than political administrations, claims to be of divine origin. Both have roots in mythology. The earliest poems immortalize gods and heroes, the notion of whose immortality comes from the obscurity of the death cult. Poetry alone can procure their salvation by casting on them the light of fame, a fame invented by the Greeks. The Romans first made political profit from poetry's unique ability to immortalize what is transient. With Virgil and Horace the history of poetry as political affirmation starts in earnest; henceforth rulers seek to ensure posthumous fame for themselves so that their subjects continue to toe the line. And to this end the poet has to be subservient to them. As a result there emerges a specific genre of poetry, the so-called eulogy of the ruler, a literary institution which has persisted to our day. Strangely, though perhaps not by accident, no one has ever undertaken a thorough investigation of this phenomenon. Here we have space only for a few hints about its history. Ancient literary theory, as we know, derived from rhetoric; after the Hellenistic period the eulogy occupied a central place in it. In accordance with the practice of professional rhetoricians, the eulogy can be traced back not to mythological origins, or to the old art of the hymn, but to the public utterances of the sophists—that is, in essence, to funeral orations and speeches in court. "It acquired political importance at the time of the Emperors. Latin and Greek eulogies of those in power were one of the sophists' main tasks. The eulogy of the ruler ($\beta\alpha\sigma\iota\lambda\iota\chi\dot{o}\varsigma$ $\lambda\dot{o}\gamma o\varsigma$) was introduced as a separate genre at that time." [2]

This had certain consequences for poetry. By the second century A.D. Hermogenes of Tarsus, one of the most important of the didactic rhetoricians, could define the genre straightforwardly as a panegyric. The technique of the eulogy of the ruler was built into a scholastic system of recurring figures of speech which, as we shall see, can be traced right into the twentieth century. The rule books of rhetoric passed on to the Middle Ages the tradition of the eulogy of the ruler. The genre spread throughout Europe, became interwoven with feudal ideas, and endured at court almost until today. The office of poet laureate still exists in England and Sweden.

In what relation does poetry stand to politics? It is obvious that anyone asking this question will find it instructive to look at the history of the eulogy of the ruler (and at its much rarer opposite, censure of the ruler), for of all the forms this relationship may take, it is in the eulogy that it appears most explicit, concrete, and undisguised.

The maxims of Walther von der Vogelweide, the earliest political poems in the German language, are a classic example of this. In the course of barely twenty years the author served three emperors: first the Hohenstaufer Philipp, then the Guelph Otto, and finally the Hohenstaufer Friedrich II. The double switch in political loyalty seems to have caused Walther little concern: without visible strain on his conscience he is ever ready to sing the praises of the victorious prince. He never hides the fact that his homage is opportunist; on the contrary, he openly declares the fact:

> *Wie solt ich den geminnen der mir übele tuot?*
> *mir muoz der iemer lieber sin der mir ist guot.*

he writes in the service of Friedrich[3] ("How shall I pay court to him who treats me ill? I cannot help preferring him who treats me well," or in plain English, I shall praise the one who knows how to reward me suitably). Such frankness must not be mistaken for naiveté; tactically it is very shrewd. *"Wirf von dir miltecliche!"* (Scatter thy bounty freely!); even the crudest poetic beggary is not adequately explained by the poet's economic dependence on the ruler whose praises he sings.[4] The shamelessness of such lines, their lack of restraint, the easy conscience with which they are uttered, all the qualities in fact which we find painful or incomprehensible in them, are characteristic. Not only do they express very clearly a fundamental relationship of feudal society, that between the lord and his vassal, a mutual dependence based on give and take; the threatening, not to say extortionary, undertone of certain verses tells us still more—the poet, despite his economic dependence, was by no means politically powerless. The prince had a fief to bestow, but the poet had fame—or the disgrace of slander, which was not to be borne lightly. The lord was quite simply dependent on the poet's praise, not out of vanity but on political grounds, as if his overlordship needed the confirmation of poetry. However incontestable the proverb that art goes a-begging, it is inadequate to explain the age-old custom of patronage, which rulers have assumed and traditionally maintained toward the fine arts, and toward poetry in particular. This patronage certainly does not owe its existence to any special liking for poets on the part of the rulers. The Maecenas-like gesture always has about it something of the pious fraud when exercised *ex officio,* since the reason for it is not the overlord's appreciation of art, or his generosity, but the fact that in the last resort it protects the protector from the protégé, from the threat to his rule inherent in poetry itself. Feudal society never lost its awareness of this, as can be seen in even the most vapid eulogistic routine, the trashiest and most servile dedicatory verses. This awareness reaches its apotheosis in a great saying, coined at the end of the feudal era. Writing to his principal, a certain Friedrich Wilhelm, who had returned some memorial verses with the comment that they were as "good as poetry," Count von Gneisenau said: "the security of the thrones is founded on poetry."

The day of this security was soon to pass. The writer of the sentence was as unaware of its historic irony as was the man to whom it was addressed; it lay in the fact that when the sentence was written it was already too late. Henceforth poetry disclosed the reverse side of that power to found and secure which it had been demonstrating since the days of Virgil—that reverse side which its patrons had always mistrusted and secretly feared: instead of the power to found, the power to shatter and overthrow; instead of affirmation, criticism. This turning point manifests itself in the crisis of the eulogy of the ruler.

Goethe did not entirely abstain from writing traditional court poetry. He undertook it as an exercise. The smooth, cold, humble verses he addressed to ruling princes (to the Emperor and Empress of Austria, for instance) betray no emotion, unless it be secret contempt; he did not include one of them in the definitive edition of his works, the *Ausgabe letzter Hand.* They were the result of an arrangement which exempted him from all public or political obligation, and were intended to insulate his own private existence from feudal society. In so far as it was not motivated by his friendship with the young Carl August, Goethe's eulogy of the ruler is an altogether nebulous production, in which we can already sense the sovereign reservations of the posthumous works:

> *Leider lässt sich noch kaum was Rechtes denken und sagen*
> *Das nicht grimmig den Staat, Götter und Sitten verletzt.*[5]

(Unfortunately there's scarcely a damn thing worth saying or thinking that doesn't in some way violate the state, the gods, or morality.)

In Germany the last poetically legitimate verses composed as eulogies of the ruler were written at the same time that Count von Gneisenau sought to draw the attention of his ruling prince to the political importance of poetry to the *ancien régime*. They are by Heinrich von Kleist. In his poem *"An Franz den Ersten, Kaiser von Östreich,"* written in 1809, we find joined once more, and for the last time, the purest forces of the genre, which the poem transcends:

> *O Herr, du trittst, der Welt ein Retter,*
> *Dem Mordgeist in die Bahn;*
> *Und wie der Sohn der duftgen Erde*
> *Nur sank, damit er stärker werde,*
> *Fällst du von neu'm ihn an!*

> *Das kommt aus keines Menschen Busen*
> *Auch aus dem deinen nicht;*
> *Das hat dem ewgen Licht entsprossen,*
> *Ein Gott dir in die Brust gegossen,*
> *Den uns're Not besticht.*

> *O sei getrost; in Klüften irgend*
> *Wächst dir ein Marmelstein;*
> *Und müsstest du im Kampf auch enden,*
> *So wirds ein anderer vollenden,*
> *Und dein der Lorbeer sein!* [6]

(Sire, by taking a stand against the spirit of evil, you have become the savior of the world; and, like the son of this fragrant earth of ours who fell but to grow in strength, you strike the murderer anew!

Your actions don't originate in any human breast, not even your own; they spring from eternal light, and it is a god who, moved by our need, has instilled it in your breast.

Be of good courage! Somewhere in some rocky cleft a block of marble bears your name; and even if it is your lot to fall in the fight, another will take your place and bring us victory—and the laurel crown will still be yours!)

The poet makes use in various ways of the aids and artifices which the rhetoric of the eulogy of the ruler has at hand: he names marble and laurel as the insignia of fame, he does not shun the obligatory mythological comparison (in this case with Antaeus), and he proclaims the prince whom he addresses as a Messiah on whose appearance depends the salvation, not of a few petty European states, but of the whole world itself. To all appearances Kleist incorporates yet another figure of speech in the poem: overlordship, like poetry, owes its existence to inspiration; both have the same origin, namely God's grace. But the God Kleist refers to has nothing in common with the ancient gods. He is not named, but he is none other than the God of history. The ruler no longer appears in person at all; not one of the verses alludes to his ancestors, his life, or his personality. Who Franz I is, the poet neither knows nor cares. The ruler is no longer Caesar, whose secret resides in his person; he is simply the viceroy of history, the executor of the *Weltgeist*. When he goes, *wirds ein anderer vollenden* (another will take your place), no matter what his name or his dynasty. Kleist's poem is a finale; it both consummates and destroys the eulogy of the ruler. Twenty-five years later Georg Büchner wrote in *Der Hessische Landbote*: "The Prince is the head of the leech that crawls over you."

This is the end of the eulogy of the ruler in German literature. The remainder of the genre, which is considerable, is either farcical or obnoxious. The countless numbers who have tried to continue it during the last hundred and fifty years have done so at the expense of their authorship. Since Kleist, every poem written in homage to those in power has backfired and exposed its author to derision or contempt. One of the many victims, and probably the most naive, was Fontane who, shortly before the turn of the century, wrote his *Wo Bismarck liegen soll*:

> *Nicht in Dom oder Fürstengruft,*
> *Er ruh' in Gottes freier Luft*
> *Draussen auf Berg und Halde,*
> *Noch besser: tief im Walde;*
> *Widukind lädt ihn zu sich ein:*
> *'Ein Sachse war er, drum ist er mein,*
> *Im Sachsenwald soll er begraben sein.'*

> *Der Leib zerfällt, der Stein zerfällt,*
> *Aber der Sachsenwald, der hält;*
> *Und kommen nach dreitausend Jahren*
> *Fremde hier des Weges gefahren*
> *Und sehen, geborgen vorm Licht der Sonnen,*

> *Den Waldgrund im Efeu tief eingesponnen*
> *Und staunen der Schönheit und jauchzen froh,*
> *So gebietet einer: "Lärmet nicht so!—*
> *Hier unten liegt Bismarck irgendwo."* 7

(No cathedral, no royal vault, shall be his resting place; he shall rest in God's fresh air, in the open on a mountain, on some hillside, or better still, deep in the forest. Widukind claims him for his own: "He was a Saxon, therefore he is mine, let him be buried in the Saxon forest."

The body decays, stone decays, but the Saxon forest lives on; and if in three thousand years strangers passing this way shall see the forest glade, sheltered from the sunlight and embedded deep in ivy, and shout for joy, astonished by its beauty, a voice will command them: "Do not shout so!—somewhere beneath this spot lies Bismarck.")

The unintended humor of these verses, particularly of the *irgendwo* (somewhere) of the last line, is proof of the disastrous impossibility of the task which Fontane, though in all good faith, set himself, the task of writing a modern eulogy of his ruler. Later attempts to revivify the genre have been less ingenuous. In face of these, irony is powerless; they are dreadful, and not only because they obliterate their authors as thinking people. There is no lack of examples. The following specimen earns an immediate place alongside the Hitler hymns of Gaiser, Seidel, and Carossa:

> *Als es geschah an jenem zweiten März,*
> *Dass leiser, immer ferner schlug sein Herz,*
> *Da war ein Schweigen wieder und ein Weinen,*
> *Um Stalins Leben bangten all die Seinen.*
>
> *Und als verhaucht sein letzter Atemzug,*
> *Da hielt die Taube ein auf ihrem Flug*
> *Und legte einen gold'nen Ölzweig nieder.*
> *Die Völker sangen stille Lieder.*
>
> *Den Namen Stalin trägt die neue Zeit.*
> *Lenin, Stalin sind Glücksunendlichkeit.*
> *Begleitet Stalin vor die Rote Mauer!*
> *Erhebt Euch in der Grösse Eurer Trauer!*
>
> *Seht! Über Stalins Grab die Taube kreist,*
> *Denn Stalin: Freiheit, Stalin: Frieden heisst.*
> *Und aller Ruhm der Welt wird Stalin heissen.*
> *Lasst uns den Ewig-Lebenden lobpreisen.*[8]

(When, on that second of March, Stalin's heartbeats grew fainter and more distant, a silence fell and there was weeping as all his people waited anxiously.

And when he had breathed his last, a passing dove, stopping in its flight, set down a golden olive branch. Meanwhile the people all sang hymns of praise to the departed.

The new era bears the name of Stalin. Lenin and Stalin stand for boundless happiness. Follow Stalin to the Red Wall! Arise in the extremity of your grief!

Look! The dove is circling Stalin's grave, for Stalin is the name of freedom, Stalin is the name for peace. And Stalin shall be the name for glory throughout the world. Let us extol him who lives eternally.)

These lines are not quoted for the disgust they are likely to arouse; for our purposes even the author, a man named Becher, is irrelevant. The lines are of interest only as a symptom. They follow Plato's precepts exactly:

And again, even if the deeds of Cronus, and his son's treatment of him, were authentic facts, it would not have been right, I should have thought, to relate them without the least reserve to young and thoughtless persons: on the contrary, it would be best to suppress them altogether. . . . Then let us not believe, any longer, or allow it to be said, that Theseus the son of Poseidon, and Peirithous the son of Zeus, went forth to commit so dire a rape; nor that any other god-sprung hero could have ventured to perpetuate such dreadful impieties as at the present day are falsely ascribed to them: rather let us oblige our poets to admit, either that the deeds in question were not their deeds, or else that they were not children of gods. . . . You must not forget that, with the single exception of hymns to the gods and panegyrics on the good, no poetry ought to be admitted into a state.[9]

In the second place, Becher's lines obey, and in no less zealous and absurdly precise a way, the old rhetorical precepts for the panegyric poem; the clichés of which it consists have one and all been played out in the course of two thousand years' usage: the olive branch, the dove, eternal life, *die Völker alle.* "An enhancement of the virtues of the person to be extolled is achieved (and has been since the early Middle Ages) by announcing that everyone joins in the admiration, joy, grief. . . . One is tempted to assert that all peoples, lands, and epochs sing X's praise." The formula "the whole world praises him" became established usage. The Carolingian poets often applied it to Karl.[10] The copybook care with which Becher, presumably unawares, has transcribed third-rate hagiographers and grammarians of the Latin middle ages is bewildering. But it cannot explain the scandal that Becher's work even exists. This scandal has nothing to do with craftsmanship; the text cannot be saved by any trick or artifice, by eliminating the stupid comparisons and falsely inflated metaphors, for instance, or by syntactical assistance. It is not the blunders that are offensive; what offends us is the actual existence of these lines.

Why? This is a question which must be thoroughly gone into, because it is fundamental. Moreover it is a question which hitherto has never been seriously asked or answered, probably because no critical effort is required to dispose of effusions which express this all too familiar fawning. They are self-condemned. One is tempted to leave it at that and save oneself the trouble of seeking a reason for this verdict. Even those who make the effort seldom go far enough. The root of the scandal does not lie where it is usually sought: it lies neither in the person of him who is praised nor him who praises.

A phenomenon such as the end of the eulogy of the ruler cannot be explained by analyzing the opinions and motives of the author, which is the method adopted everywhere during recent decades when the relationship of poetry to politics has been discussed. This method itself needs explanation. In view of the experience we have had with our literature, it is understandable that we have grown accustomed to question the political "reliability" or even the "respectability" of a writer, but the very terminology of such questioning shows that it threatens to infect criticism with the totalitarian stuff of its mortal enemies.

To point to the party badges, loyal addresses, and public positions of certain authors can provide data for criticism, but nothing more; it doesn't enable us to form a judgment of their work. No poem by Benn, not a single Heidegger sentence, can be refuted in this manner—which statement doesn't excuse the slightest act of barbarity. We have not made it to exonerate from criticism Hitler's and Stalin's spokesmen. On the contrary, our intention is first and foremost to subject them to a criticism which does not take its task too lightly. We have only to question the motives that prompted Becher, for instance, to write his hymn to Stalin to forget all claim to critical acumen. Whether he wrote it out of stupidity or opportunism, voluntarily or under duress, is completely beside the point. The same applies to the sentiments in Becher's heart: pious conviction or cynical winking, laborious self-deception or augurlike humbug—it is of equally small importance. Eulogy of the ruler and poetry are incompatible: this proposition is as true of Fontane as it is of Becher, and it is independent of the person of the author who violates it, whatever his motives or sentiments.

It is also independent of the subject of eulogy. Any explanation that concentrates on the person praised is also inadequate. Becher's lines are not disqualified by Stalin's crimes; it is enough that they are addressed to a ruler at all. Comparison with Fontane's harmless and labored production is instructive also in this respect. Poetry can no longer be addressed to any statesman, no matter what our opinion of him. Poetry addressed to Adenauer is equally unimaginable, as much a contradiction in terms as if it were addressed to Hitler, Kennedy, or de Gaulle. The phenomenon in question cannot be grasped in ideological or moral terms. It is not merely the fact that no writer of any importance has made such an attempt of his own free will that supports this conclusion. The argument can be demonstrated *ex contrario:* with the possibility of eulogizing the ruler has also gone the possibility of defaming him. Heine realized this.[11] No legitimate poetic work exists in which Hitler's name has been preserved. Even Brecht came to grief in his attempt to defame him in verse, as he also did in his poem *"Die Erziehung der Hirse,"* in which Stalin is mentioned, and in *"Kantate zu Lenin's Todestag."* [12]

This failure is first and last of a political nature. It is not because of a general compulsion towards abstraction, for instance, that true poetry resists both eulogy and defamation of the ruler. Nor is it the fact that they are mentioned by name which renders worthless all the poems on Hitler and Stalin; poetry does not reject names in general, it rejects only the names of those exercising authority. Poems addressed to anyone else are as possible today as ever—poems to a wife, a friend, a taxi driver, a greengrocer. Many modern poems are addressed to people: Lorca lamented the bullfighter Ignacio Sanches Majías in an oratorio, Supervielle wrote an ode to

Lautréamont, and Auden a memorial to Yeats; none of these names is rejected by the language of poetry, they are all incorporated in the text without breaking it up.[13]

What have we accomplished with these reflections? The end of the eulogy of the ruler, that is, of an extreme political element in poetry, defies all political, psychological, or sociological explanations. We are concerned with an objective fact: the language of poetry refuses its services to anyone who uses it to immortalize the names of those exercising power. The reason for this refusal lies in poetry itself, not outside it. With this conclusion we have reached a decisive stage in our discussion and we can now drop the example of the eulogy of the ruler, which we have used to prie open the surface beneath which lies the secret of what binds poetry to politics and what divorces it from it.

Our example teaches us that the political aspect of poetry must be immanent in poetry itself and cannot be derived from outside it. This completely condemns Marxist literary doctrine as it has conceived of itself up to this point. That doctrine's attempts to isolate the political content of a poetic work resemble sieges. The poem is encircled from without; the stronger the poem, the more difficult it is to force it to surrender. What are the author's class origins? How has he voted? What marks do his ideological utterances earn? Who has paid him? What public has he written for? Has he spent his life in castles or hovels? Were his friends millionaires or stevedores? What has he supported, what opposed? Justifiable questions, highly interesting questions, frequently neglected questions, instructive, useful questions—only they do not touch the heart of the matter, don't even want to. The literary critic who writes from the standpoint of literary sociology is blind to his subject and sees only what lies at the surface, and he betrays his opinion of the quality of the works he criticizes at once with the choice of his categories. Hence his predilection for the classics; this enables him to avoid the vexing question of the status of the work into which he is inquiring. From its beginnings, Marxist criticism has unhesitatingly accepted the judgments of the bourgeois literary canon, contenting itself with using them for its own purpose. The reverse of this "cultivation of our heritage" is disastrous uncertainty in the face of contemporary production. Marx expressed a considered opinion on only one novel of his day, a fairly trivial work by Eugene Sue called *The Secrets of Paris*.[14] The theory of realism developed by Engels starts with a discussion of a long-forgotten English penny dreadful.[15]

Only in connection with Ferdinand Lassalle's play *Franz von Sickingen* do Marx and Engels have anything to say on the subject of tragedy; they make no mention of Büchner's work, which appeared during the same decade.[16] A hundred years later Georg Lukács was to treat the literary output of his day with the same lack of discrimination: on the chessboard of his theory of realism he valiantly opposes Romain Rolland and Theodore Dreiser to Proust, Joyce, Kafka, and Faulkner, without even suspecting that such a match of pawns against kings might expose the promoter to ridicule.[17] Fortunately neither Marx nor Lukács has expressed his opinion on poetry, and we can only guess what the world has been spared. For while orthodox literary sociology can at least enter halfway into the heart of a novel or play, by way of the *pons asinorum* of its plot, poetry excludes such an approach from the outset. The only approach to poetry is via language, and this is why Lukács ignores poetry.

Such obtuseness plays into the hands of the bourgeois esthetic which would like to deny poetry any social aspect. Too often the champions of inwardness and sensibility are reactionaries. They consider politics a special subject best left to professionals, and wish to detach it completely from all other human activity. They advise poetry to stick to such models as they have devised for it, in other words, to high aspirations and eternal values. The promised reward for this continence is timeless validity. Behind these high-sounding proclamations lurks a contempt for poetry no less profound than that of vulgar Marxism. For a political quarantine placed on poetry in the name of eternal values, itself serves political ends. Poetry is to be made surreptitiously serviceable to these ends precisely where its social relevance is denied, as decoration, as window dressing, as a stage set representing eternity. Both sides, both Weidle and Lukács for example, agree that poetry in essence, and especially modern poetry, is disturbing and that it does not fit into the plans of either of them because it is no one's handmaiden.

The confusion of ideas is general and almost total. In the search for enemies or allies, the diaries and letters, opinions, and lives of the poets are gone over with a fine-tooth comb, and the fact that they have also been engaged in writing poetry becomes practically superfluous. The following are examples of this hopeless confusion.

Insofar as it is possible to speak of progressive literary criticism in our country, those practicing it have always regarded German romanticism as a purely reactionary movement.[18] These critics have heard that the romantics counted landed gentry and anti-Semites among them, but they remain unaware that Novalis and Brentano, those politically irresponsible sons of the German middle class, gave birth to a poetic revolution that was the beginning of modernity, a revolution without which the writings of Trakl, Brecht, Heym, and Stadler, Benn, Arp, Apollinaire, Éluard, Lorca, Neruda, Jessenin, Mandelstamm, Eliot, and Thomas cannot be imagined. These critics have been content to interrogate romanticism ideologically, to denounce it as a counterrevolutionary movement, and thus to deliver an indispensable and powerful element of modern tradition to nationalism and subsequently to fascism. On the other hand, they have given high progressive marks to Herwegh, Freiligrath, and Weerth, to men, that is, whose poetry was mediocre and epigonous. The results can still be seen in the handsomely bound, allegedly revolutionary lyric writing practiced in Dresden and Leipzig today.

Or take the opposite case of a German right-wing critic who mistakes for a general world condition the sluggish intellectual climate of the Federal Republic (he calls it "postrevolutionary," thereby indicating that his notion of revolution is limited to Hitlerism); in 1961 this bourgeois critic tried to claim Baudelaire and Eliot as good conservatives for his dwindling company by playing off the reactionary views of these writers against their revolutionary works. It is true that in his diary Baudelaire wrote the horrifying phrase, *"Belle conspiration à organiser pour l'extermination de la Race Juive,"* [19] but does this turn *Les Fleurs du Mal* into a collection of SS sermons? T.S. Eliot acknowledged the monarchy and the Anglican Church; does *The Waste Land* thereby become an edifying plea for a literature of the day before yesterday? Can a confining political viewpoint of the author cast the poetic revolt of these verses into chains? Since Plato's day, of course, the self-appointed ideological watchdogs have always considered viewpoints more important than the objective social content of poetry. This content can be found only in the language of poetry, the discovery of which presupposes an ear.

Under such auspices the expression "political poem" becomes suspect to the point where it is no longer of any use. Everyone imagines he knows what it means, but on closer examination we find that it is applied almost exclusively to writings serving the ends either of agitation or of the establishment. But what we have learned from the example of the eulogy of the ruler holds true in this instance too. The results can be classified under battle songs and marching songs, poster rhymes and hymns, propaganda chants and manifestoes in verse—irrespective of whose or what interests they are intended to promote. Either they are useless for the purposes of those who commission them or they have nothing to do with poetry. No national anthem written in the twentieth century is a legitimate poem; it is impossible to write such an anthem. The attempt is punishable by ridicule. If we are unwilling to admit this, we have only to compare two such attempts from the recent German past:

> *Aufgestanden aus Ruinen*
> *Und der Zukunft zugewandt,*
> *Lass uns dir zum Guten dienen*
> *Deutschland, einig Vaterland.*[20]

(Risen from ruins, turned toward the future, let us serve your welfare, Germany, common Fatherland.)

This is a verse from the East German national anthem, composed by Johannes R. Becher in 1950. For the Federal Republic, on the other hand, Rudolf Alexander Schröder proposed the following lines, although in fact they were rejected by the authorities in favor of the proven and ever-topical words of Fallersleben:

> *Land der Liebe, Vaterland,*
> *Heilger Grund, auf den sich gründet,*
> *Was in Lieb und Leid verbündet*
> *Herz mit Herzen, Hand mit Hand:*
> *Frei wie wir dir angehören,*
> *Schling um uns dein Friedensband,*
> *Land der Liebe, Vaterland!* [21]

(Land of love, Fatherland! Sacred ground on which everything is founded that unites us in love and sorrow, heart to heart, hand to hand: Free as we belong to you and pledge ourselves to you, wrap your band of peace around us, land of love, Fatherland!)

Despite the ideological differences that separate the two authors, their works are interchangeable. Phrasing, prosody, and vocabulary are identical. In neither case can one really speak of a political poem, since these anthems bear no more relation to poetry than does an advertising slogan for margarine. They fulfill their political mission by lies. Contrast with them a poem by Brecht, *"Der Radwechsel"* (Changing the Wheel):

> *Ich sitze am Strassenhang.*
> *Der Fahrer wechselt das Rad.*
> *Ich bin nicht gern, wo ich herkomme.*
> *Ich bin nicht gern, wo ich hinfahre.*
> *Warum sehe ich den Radwechsel*
> *Mit Ungeduld?* [22]

(I sit by the roadside. The driver changes the wheel. I don't like where I came from. I don't like where I'm going. Why am I impatient as I watch him change the wheel?)

A political poem? The mere question shows how little is to be gained by the use of that category. A wheel is being changed—six lines in which neither the Fatherland nor any other regime is mentioned, six lines before which the zeal of the ideological carpers falters. They too regard "Changing the Wheel" with impatience, because they cannot use the poem for their purposes. It says nothing to them, because it says too much. It was written in the summer of 1953. A political poem or not? This is a verbal quibble. If politics means taking part in the social conditions that men create for themselves in history, then *"Der Radwechsel,"* like every poem worthy of the name, is political in essence. If politics means the use of power for the purposes of those who wield it, then Brecht's lines, in common with poetry of any kind, have nothing to do with it. The poem expresses in an exemplary way the fact that it is not at the disposal of politics: this is its political content.

Which proves what? That we cannot exhaust this turbid theme by resorting to clear-cut linear theses. Looking at the subject of poetry and politics as a whole, and not from the view of an individual poem, we do not have much to go on that is simple. It is necessary to insist on what there is, not because it is new but because, being well known, it is constantly being forgotten: poetry and politics are not "specialized fields" but historic processes, one in the medium of speech, the other in the medium of power. Both are integral parts of history. As sociology, literary criticism cannot see that language constitutes the social character of poetry, and not its entanglement in the political battle. Bourgeois literary esthetics is blind to, or else conceals, the fact that poetry is essentially social. The answers offered by the two doctrines to the question of the relationship of the poetic to the political process are correspondingly clumsy and useless: complete dependence in one case, complete independence in the other. On the one hand is the party calendar, on the other timelessness. The real question at issue remains unexamined and indeed unasked; for what remains to be said we are forced to rely on conjectures and postulates; we have no scholarship to help us.

"Owing to inclement weather the German revolution occurred in music." [23] This bitterly sarcastic remark of Tucholsky's, urgently recommended as a motto for our political historians, reveals more than is apparent at first sight—more perhaps than its author intended. It is not only in politics that revolutions take place.

"The overseers of the state must hold fast to . . . the principle . . . which forbids any innovation, in either gymnastics or music, upon the established order, requiring it, on the contrary, to be most strictly maintained. . . . For the introduction of a new kind of music must be shunned as imperilling the whole state; since styles of music are never disturbed without affecting the most important political institutions. . . ."

"Then to all appearances," I continued, "it is here in music that our guardians should erect their guardhouse."

"At any rate," said he, "it is here that lawlessness easily creeps in unawares."

"Yes, in the guise of amusement, and professing to do no mischief."

"No, and it does none, except that gradually gaining a lodgement, it quietly insinuates itself into manners and customs; and from these it issues in greater force, and makes its way into mutual compacts; and from compacts it goes on to attack laws and constitutions, displaying the utmost impudence, Socrates, until it ends by overturning everything, both in public and in private." [24]

No enemy of poetry has described its effects with greater insight than Plato: unpredictable effects, calculable by no one, not even by the poet, like those of a trace element or a shower of tiny spores. Plato's warnings are more perceptive than any literary scholarship to date; they relate not to manifest political opinions and content but to the heart of the poetic process, which threatens to elude the guardians' control; its political consequences are never more dangerous than where it doesn't even try to serve as a guideline for poetic conduct.

Despite their barbaric ignorance, Plato's totalitarian followers have displayed a surer instinct for this connection than have the professional estheticians; their official bodies have forbidden, as a danger to the state, not only tendencies and contents but, to use Plato's language, "styles" and "modes," that is, deviations in poetic language itself. Only a few years ago, the politburo of a small Central European state rendered a poet the macabre homage of forcing him to alter the punctuation he had chosen for his writings; he was enjoined, for reasons of state, to put back the full stops and commas he had left out. We are ill-advised to laugh at this. The incident, however unimportant it may seem, brings to our attention something that, while literally true, often remains unnoticed, although it is talked about at every cultural street corner: there are conservative and revisionist, revolutionary and reactionary impulses in poetry itself. What do these words mean when applied to the poetic process? If we wish to wrest them from idle talk and instill a little precision in them we must turn not to ideological reactions but to works, not to viewpoint but to language. Many a country squire loyal to the crown will then appear as a revolutionary, many a political Jacobin as a poetic obscurantist. It seems reasonable to suppose that the revolutionary process of poetry develops in quiet, anonymous homes rather than at congresses where booming bards announce world revolutions in the language of the poeticizing birdwatcher.

If we want to gain a deeper insight into what binds poetry to politics and what divorces the two from each other, we cannot hope for proof, nor can we proceed without risk; in other words, we are dependent on speculations. In conclusion, we submit three theses concerning the development of the poetic process in history, and the relationship between it and the political process:

1. Poetry must be more incorrupt than ever in insisting on its birthright against all domination. What distinguishes the poetic from the political process has been growing clearer over the last hundred years. The greater the pressure to which poetry is subjected, the clearer this difference becomes. Its political mission is to refuse any political mission and to continue to speak for everyone about things of which no one speaks, of a tree, a stone, of that which does not exist. This is the most difficult of missions. None is easier to forget. There is no one to demand an accounting; on the contrary, the man

who betrays his mission to the interests of those in authority is rewarded. But in poetry there are no extenuating circumstances. A poem that offers itself for sale, whether in error or from baseness, is condemned to death; there is no reprieve.

2. Authority, stripped of its mythical cloak, can no longer be reconciled with poetry. What used to be called inspiration is now called criticism, which becomes the productive restlessness of the poetic process. In the eyes of authority, which can recognize no ἀρχή other than itself, poetry is anarchistic, intolerable because not at authority's disposal, subversive in its very existence. Its mere presence is an indictment of government announcements and the scream of propaganda, of manifestoes and banners. Its critical function is simply that of the child in the fairy tale. No "political engagement" is necessary to see that the emperor is wearing no clothes. It is enough that a single verse breaks the speechless howl of applause.

3. Poetry transmits the future. In the face of what is currently established, it speaks what is obvious and unrealized. Francis Ponge has said that he writes his poems as if he were writing on the day following a successful revolution. This is true of all poetry. Poetry is anticipating, even when it takes the form of doubt, rejection, or negation. It is not that it speaks of the future, but that it speaks as if a future were possible, as if free speech were possible among people not free, as if there were no alienation, no inarticulateness (since inarticulateness cannot express itself and alienation cannot communicate itself). Were it not at the same time criticism, such an anticipation would prove poetry a lie; were it not in the same breath anticipation, such criticism would be impotent. The path of poetry is narrow and menaced with dangers, its chance of success modest—no less modest, even if more distinct, than our own.

Translated by Michael Roloff

Commonplaces on the newest literature

> Josephine exerts herself, a mere nothing in voice, a mere nothing in execution, she asserts herself and gets across to us; it does us good to think of that. A really trained singer, if ever such a one should be found among us, we could certainly not endure at such a time and we should unanimously turn away from the senselessness of any such performance. May Josephine be spared from perceiving that the mere fact of our listening to her is proof that she is not a singer. . . .
>
> Josephine's road, however, must go downhill. The time will soon come when her last notes sound and die into silence. She is a small episode in the eternal history of our people, and the people will get over the loss of her.
>
> Franz Kafka, *Josephine the Singer, or the Mouse Folk.*

So now we can hear it tolling again, the little death nell for literature. However, it isn't tin wreaths with which it is being laid to rest. As a matter of fact, the invitations to the burial are legion. The funeral banquets, so we hear, are exceedingly well attended: they are a hit at the Book Fair. The mourners don't appear overly downcast. Rather, a manic exuberance seems to be taking hold, a slightly heady fury. The few oddballs off in the corner don't seriously disturb the festivities. They are making their trip on their own, perhaps with a little tea in their pipe.

The funeral procession leaves behind a dust cloud of theories, little of which is new. The literati are celebrating the end of literature. The poets prove to themselves and others the impossibility of making poetry. The critics extol the passing of criticism. The sculptors produce plastic coffins for their plastics. The event as a whole takes for itself the appellation "cultural revolution," but it has more the look of a country fair.

2. *Period of deliberation.* Almost everyone longs for certainty; and if indeed it is all over and done with for writing, the fact evidently would be a kind of soporific. But the relief of one group is as premature as the glee and panic of the others. Old habits die hard; poets incarnate can scarcely be reformed through vociferous cold-turkey treatments; the loudness of the saw conceals how thick the branch is on which literature sits.

Also worth contemplating: the "death of literature" itself is a literary metaphor, and scarcely of recent vintage. For at least a hundred years, say since the days of Lautréamont, the victim who has been pronounced dead has in fact found itself in a permanent state of agony, and like bourgeois society itself has known how to make its own crisis the basis of its existence. Its interment is an event without a foreseeable end, during which the mummy keeps popping up with ominous freshness in better fettle each time and more highly rouged.

The mourners stay in each other's company—that is, in the minority. As regards the masses, they have other worries. They take about as much notice of the death of literature, which has never gotten as far as the newsstand, as they did of its life. Not even the book business needs be concerned; because at seven in the morning when the deceased is having her beauty rest, the world is back in kilter.

Nonetheless, despite the dumb theses, the broken-winded

intermezzi, and the monotonous bleating which accompany them, a mere shrug of the shoulder by the rest of us would be too little in face of the obsequies. For the mood on which they are based and which they cannot articulate runs deep. The symptoms of the illness cannot be simply dismissed. Not only is contemporary production hit by it, making self-doubt the dominating feature of its esthetic; but discomfort, impatience, and disgust have seized the writers and the readers, which—for the Second German Republic at least—is new and unheard of. Both suddenly understand what has always been the case: that literature, perhaps even more than other products, is at the mercy of the laws of the market place. However, since production of literature is much less easily controlled through a monopolistic administration than is the production of margarine, such an insight puts the whole enterprise into question. Deliver, consume; deliver, consume: that is the imperative of the market; when writers and readers notice that those who deliver are swallowed and those who swallow are delivered up, this leads to a congestion.

It is this very elitist character of our literature which makes it susceptible to such seizures. It can only operate undisturbed as long as it is unaware of its own situation. Since literature is made by the few for the few, it takes little to disturb this equilibrium. When the brightest heads between twenty and thirty are more interested in an agitation model than an "experimental text"; when they prefer to use faktographs to picaresque novels; when they sneer at literature, both its production and consumption—these are indeed promising signs. But they must be understood.

3. *Local paper.* Someone from whose lips the word "age" slips a little too easily and who wants to pronounce statements about literature *qua* literature may get his tongue caught in the process. Premature globalization usually conceals the specifics of a situation, and these are what should be clarified. A few provisional pieces of information may perhaps be gained by localizing the problem.

Since World War II West German society has assigned a

peculiar role to "cultural life" and to literature in particular. A leading journal of the postwar period was called *Die Wandlung* (Transformation). The mandate of German literature after 1945 has been to demonstrate to the Germans, and even more to the outside world, such a transformation. The less thought was given to real social changes, to the rearrangements of power and ownership conditions, the more indispensable became for West German society an alibi in the superstructure. Very different motives came together here in a new-fangled amalgamation:

The wish to compensate, at least intellectually, for the complete bankruptcy of the German Reich;

The evidently urgent need, regardless of the great collective crime, to once again be regarded as a "cultured people";

The hunger of a state, devoid of such, for prestige of any kind;

The sufficiently well-known "idealism" which wanted to assuage its bad conscience in the face of rising mass consumption with atavistic antipathies to civilization;

A form of anti-fascism which satisfies itself with having better taste than the Nazis, and which manifested its democratic mentality by buying what the former called "degenerate": pictures on which nothing can be recognized and poems with nothing in them.

The need to be at least esthetically "with it" in the world, the wish to be classy enough to make it in world cultural circles—this objective was most recently achieved with *The Tin Drum*.

There's one point these factors have in common: they have heaped exonerating and surrogate functions on a literature which of course was unequipped to cope with them. Literature was supposed to take the place of a void in the Federal Republic—the absence of a genuine political life. Thus the restoration was opposed as though it was a literary phenomenon, that is with literary means; opposition could be repressed into the book reviews; revolutions in poetry were the substitute for the nonoccurrence of revolutions in the social structure; artistic avant-garde was to conceal political regression. And the more West German society stabilized itself, the more urgently it asked for social criticism in literature; the fewer results the writer's engagement produced, the louder the clamor for it. This mechanism secured literature an uncontested place in society, but it also led to self-deceptions which seem grotesque today.

The rise of this literature was bought with an optimism that was blind to theory, with a naive presumptuousness and an increasing incompatibility of political demand with political practice. And so there was no avoiding the inevitable hangover. When the totality of imperialism became evident, when social contradictions could no longer be covered up, when politics took to the street, the cracks began to show through the cultural façade. What had "engaged" itself for twenty years now saw itself confronted by alternatives which no longer bore the initials of the parties in Bonn. Freshly baked writers of "classics" who had become accustomed to reading their position papers in front of the TV cameras with the aplomb of ministers of health suddenly found themselves —stupefied and peeved—confronted by a public which rewarded their sermons with salvos of laughter. However, if what succumbed to its own fictions was literature, it has indeed long since ceased to suffer.

4. *The old questions, the old answers.* However, the dilemma in which literature, like all the arts, finds itself is deeper and older than our local obsessions. In any event, at the latest by 1968, it was realized that the dilemma cannot be solved with phrases. Kafka's story of the singer Josephine dates to 1924. Six years later André Breton wrote: "In the area about whose specific expressive possibilities you are enquiring (namely the artistic and literary production) my thinking can only oscillate between the awareness of its complete autonomy and that of its strict dependence." And he develops this contradiction with the demand for a literature which is simultaneously "conditional and unconditional, utopian and realistic, which sees its purpose only in itself and wants nothing but to serve."

The surrealists made the squaring of the circle into a program. They committed themselves unreservedly to the cause of the communist world revolution and simultaneously maintained their intellectual sovereignty, the autonomy of their literary criteria. As the foundation of this attitude, Breton invoked the lawfulness of a "poetic determinism" which is as inescapable as that of dialectical materialism. In today's discussion the same matter bears a different tag. There is talk about the "objective state of the genre," and of "artistic compulsion"—categories which bear suspicious resemblance to the "material compulsion" to which the administrators of the status quo hold fast.

The surrealists' attempt to establish themselves in their dilemma as though it was a citadel had something stubbornly heroic about it; the same cannot be said of their successors, the dispersed troops of the neo-avant-garde. The confessions of revolutionary positions which one can hear from some authors of the Tel-quel group in Paris, the Gruppo 63 in Italy, and the Noigandres-Circle in Brazil have sacrificed every connection with their literary production, which shows no structural differences from the work of other authors who avoid any form of political engagement or are openly reactionary. Evidently the "material compulsion" to which this literature feels obligated succeeds in asserting itself, despite the subjective insights, as a kind of literary meta-ideology of which there is no escaping for these authors.

This ideology avoids any social content. It is technocratic. Its concept of progress aims at means of production, not at production relationships, which is why their products remain ambiguous; and it is scarcely accidental that concepts like *indeterminacy, accident,* and *gratuitousness* play such a central role in their esthetic. The manufacturers of such a literature may be subjectively honest when they mouth the word "revolution"; but of necessity they move into the proximity of industrial technocrats like Servan-Schreiber.

A literature which thinks of itself as a mere instrument of agitation is antithetical to the technocratic avant-garde. Regis Debray, in a letter from Bolivia, pleaded with great decisive-

ness, if also in the tone of traditional poetic noblesse, for such
a literature:

For the fight which is being fought before our eyes and within each
of us, the fight between prehistory and the wish to live in accordance
with our idea of what it means to be a human being, we need works
which give testimony of that: we need rage and screams, we need the
sum of all actions of which such works give us news. Only when we
have them, indispensable and simple reports, songs for the march,
cries for help and watchwords of the day, only then do we have
the right to take pleasure in beautiful literary products.

A literature that corresponds to such demands does not
exist, at least not in Europe. All attempts so far to break out
of the ghetto of cultural life and "to reach the masses," for
example, by means of agit-prop songs and street theater, have
been defeated. They proved literarily irrelevant and politically ineffective. Of course this is not a question of talent.
Those who are addressed, even if they cannot give articulate
account of why, see effortlessly through the bad immediacy,
the helpless mental short-circuiting, the self-deception of such
attempts, and sense it as a form of ingratiation. On this subject too, Breton said the necessary thing already forty years
ago: "I don't believe in the present possibility of a literary
art which can express the endeavors of the working class. I
have good reason to refuse to consider something of that kind
possible. For in a prerevolutionary epoch the writers or artists
are necessarily rooted in the bourgeoisie and, if only for that
reason, are incapable of finding the language to express the
needs of the proletariat."

5. *Omnivorous*. This, half a century after the October Revolution, needs a few additions. The Soviet Union so far lacks
a revolutionary literature, too. (Mayakovsky remained an exception; the literary avant-garde of the Russian twenties primarily propagated and radicalized bourgeois poetics; the
spread of the "cultural heritage" which is now indeed available to a large majority of Soviet citizens may be regarded as
a socialist accomplishment, however it rests on an exclusively

quantitative conception of culture which derives from old social democratic traditions and on an entirely retrospective interpretation of the slogan "Art for the people." A revolutionary culture cannot be founded on such premises, as the present condition of Soviet literature shows only too clearly.)

To this day the products of the bourgeois epoch in world literature set the tone, determine the operative criteria, the existing possibilities, the usual conflicts and the increasing contradictions. Bourgeois in origin are socialist realism and abstract poetry, literature as affirmation and literature of protest, absurd and documentary theater. Culture is the sole area in which the bourgeoisie rules uncontested, and the end of this rule is not in sight.

On the other hand, the importance of literature in the class struggle has diminished since the nineteenth century. Although it was impossible to separate them neatly, it was always possible to distinguish between two elements from the very beginning. As the ruling literature was, on the one hand, also the literature of the ruling class, it had to serve the consolidation of class rule and its camouflaging. On the other hand, it is a product of a revolution and, inasmuch as it has remained loyal to this origin, it has transgressed the limits of its mandate. Its function in the class struggle therefore was a double one from the beginning: it served mystification but also enlightenment. These functions, however, on which a criticism of literature could also orient itself decisively, have obviously been atrophying, at least since the end of World War I. Since that time imperialism has developed such mighty instruments for the industrial manipulation of consciousness that it is no longer dependent on literature. Vice versa, literature's critical function has also kept shrinking. Already in the thirties Walter Benjamin could ascertain "that the bourgeois production and publication apparatus can assimilate, even propagate, an astonishing mass of revolutionary themes without putting its own existence into serious doubt." Since then the capacity of the capitalist society to reabsorb, suck up, swallow "cultural goods" of widely varying digestibility has enormously increased. Today the political harmlessness of all literary, indeed, all artistic products, is clearly evident: the very fact that they can be defined as such neutralized them. Their claim to be enlightening, their utopian surplus, their critical potential has shriveled to mere appearance.

Precisely analogous to this emaciation of the social content is the assimilation of their formal inventions by late capitalist society. Even the most extreme esthetic contraventions no longer meet with serious resistance. A percentage of the season ticket holders of course are against them. But sooner or later, and usually sooner, by way of detours via advertising, design, and styling the inventions become part and parcel of the consumer sphere. This means the end of an equivocation which has ruled progressive literature for fifty years: the parallelism or even equation of formal and social innovation.

A critical rhetoric which transposes the concept of revolution to esthetic categories was only possible at a time when breaking with the conventions of writing (painting, composing, etc.) could still be regarded as a challenge. This time is now over. Proclamations and manifestoes announcing "revolts," "revolutions" of language, syntax, metaphor sound hollow today. It is not by accident that they meet with well-meaning understanding from the ruling institutions and are correspondingly remunerated.

What does it take to be a . . . *revolutionary?* From our experience with thousands of applicants we know that not everyone is suited to be an independent salesman. But we also know that there are thousands of able men who don't have the opportunity to develop themselves because of the limitations of their present income.

The world-renowned Chase Group, one of whose by no means insignificant subsidiaries is the Securities Management Corporation, was founded in Boston in 1932. It offers a solid, even conservative, solution for long-term investments to small as well as large investors. Scientific analysts of the first rank insure a sensible aggressiveness of capital growth.

If you are revolutionary enough to work exclusively on a commission basis and work particularly hard the first few months you will create for yourself a winning existence with a winner's income.— Job offer in a German daily, summer 1968.

6. *Not responsible for personal property.* I summarize: a revolutionary literature does not exist unless it be in a completely vapid sense of the word. This has objective reasons which writers are in no position to alter. Literary works cannot be assigned an essential social function under present conditions. From this it follows that one also cannot find usable criteria for judging their social function. Hence a literary criticism which tries to do more than belch forth its personal preferences and which could regulate the market is not possible.

These findings appear lapidary. Therefore one should not forget that one cannot base a wholesale judgment of contemporary literature on them. The sentence that one cannot attribute a cogent social function to literature, regarded logically, makes no new certainties available to us. It denies that there are such certainties. And if that is indeed the case, it points to a risk which from now on is part of the composing of poems, stories, and dramas: the risk that such works are useless and futile, regardless of their artistic success or failure. Whoever makes literature as art isn't disproved by this, but he cannot feel justified either.

If I am right, if no verdict is possible on writing, all the revolutionary haranguing, which looks for relief from its own impotence in the liquidation of literature, won't accomplish anything either. A political movement which, instead of attacking the power of the state, tangles with aging belletrists would only manifest its own cowardice in this manner. If we have a literature that exists merely on the basis of a wild guess, if basically there is no making out whether writing still contains an element, if only the slightest, of the future, that is, if irrelevance constitutes the social essence of this kind of work, then a cultural revolution can neither be made with or against it. Instead of shouting "Hands up!" to the producers of slim volumes, the militant groups should attack the cultural apparatuses whose social function—in contrast to that of poetry and prose—is only too clearly recognizable and without whose rule ruling has become inconceivable. However, these apparatuses aren't impotent opponents against whom the Left can turn its fear, its puritanism, and its philistinism into aggression without actually risking something.

7. *Writing and reading, oyez.* For writers who cannot become accustomed to their irrelevance (and how many is that?) I only have modest, even paltry, suggestions. What is evidently the most difficult job, an appropriate estimate of our significance, would presumably be to our advantage. Nothing is won if we let ourselves be consumed by doubt and intimidated by rhythmic chants, and substitute for the traditional air of importance a newly practiced gesture of humility. In a society where political illiteracy celebrates triumphs, it should not be all that difficult for people who can read and write to find limited but useful occupations. That is certainly not a new task. Börne began to work at it 150 years ago in Germany, and Rosa Luxemburg has been dead for fifty years already. What we have today, measured against these models, makes a modest impression: for example, Günther Wallraff's reports from German factories, Bahman Nirumand's book on Persia, Ulrike Meinhoff's columns, Georg Alsheimer's Vietnam report. I consider the use of such works uncontestable. The discrepancy between the task which they set themselves and the results they have achieved cannot be reduced to a question of talent. It is to be traced back to the production relationship of the mind industry, which the alphabetizers have been incapable of outplaying to date. The authors hold fast to the traditional means: the book, individual authorship, the distribution limits of the market, the separation of theoretical and practical work. A counter example is the work of Fritz Teufel.[1] Other possibilities which are less personality-bound have to be thought up and tested.

The political alphabetization of Germany is an immense project. Like every other undertaking, it should of course start with the alphabetization of the alphabetizers. This itself is a protracted and tortuous process. Furthermore, every such enterprise depends on the principle of mutuality. Only those are suited for it who continually learn from those who learn from them. That incidentally is one of the most pleasant sides of the business which I mean. The writer who lets himself get involved in this suddenly feels critical reciprocity, a feedback between reader and writer of which he could not have dreamed as a belletrist. Instead of moronic reviews which certify that he has developed promisingly from his second to third book but that his fourth has been a bitter disappointment, he now finds corrections, resistance, curses, counter proof—in one word, consequences. And what is said to him is usable, can become practice, even mutual practice. These consequences are fragmentary and temporary. They are isolated. But there is no real reason for their remaining so. Perhaps the alphabetizer will one day achieve what was denied him while he sought to make art: that the utilitarian value of his work outgrows its market value.

8. *Calendar saying.* "There are no worms in the door hinges."

Translated by Michael Roloff

Constituents of a theory of the media

> If you should think this is Utopian, then I would ask you to consider why it is Utopian.
>
> Brecht: *Theory of Radio*

With the development of the electronic media, the industry that shapes consciousness has become the pacemaker for the social and economic development of societies in the late industrial age. It infiltrates into all other sectors of production, takes over more and more directional and control functions, and determines the standard of the prevailing technology.

In lieu of normative definitions, here is an incomplete list of new developments which have emerged in the last twenty years: news satellites, color television, cable relay television, cassettes, videotape, videotape recorders, video-phones, stereophony, laser techniques, electrostatic reproduction processes, electronic high-speed printing, composing and learning machines, microfiches with electronic access, printing by radio, time-sharing computers, data banks. All these new forms of media are constantly forming new connections both with each other and with older media like printing, radio, film, television, telephone, teletype, radar, and so on. They are clearly coming together to form a universal system.

The general contradiction between productive forces and productive relationships emerges most sharply, however, when they are most advanced. By contrast, protracted structural crises, as in coal mining, can be solved merely by getting rid of a backlog, that is to say, essentially they can be solved within the terms of their own system, and a revolutionary strategy that relied on them would be shortsighted.

Monopoly capitalism develops the consciousness-shaping industry more quickly and more extensively than other sectors of production; it must at the same time fetter it. A socialist media theory has to work at this contradiction, demonstrate that it cannot be solved within the given productive relationships—rapidly increasing discrepancies, potential destructive forces. "Certain demands of a prognostic nature must be made" of any such theory (Benjamin).

A "critical" inventory of the status quo is not enough. There is danger of underestimating the growing conflicts in the media field, of neutralizing them, of interpreting them merely in terms of trade unionism or liberalism, on the lines of traditional labor struggles or as the clash of special interests (program heads/executive producers, publishers/authors, monopolies/medium sized businesses, public corporations/private companies, etc.). An appreciation of this kind does not go far enough and remains bogged down in tactical arguments.

So far there is no Marxist theory of the media. There is therefore no strategy one can apply in this area. Uncertainty, alternations between fear and surrender, mark the attitude of the socialist Left to the new productive forces of the media industry. The ambivalence of this attitude merely mirrors the ambivalence of the media themselves without mastering it. It could only be overcome by releasing the emancipatory potential which is inherent in the new productive forces—a potential which capitalism must sabotage just as surely as Soviet revisionism, because it would endanger the rule of both systems.

THE MOBILIZING POWER OF THE MEDIA

2. The open secret of the electronic media, the decisive political factor, which has been waiting, suppressed or crippled, for its moment to come, is their mobilizing power.

When I say *mobilize* I mean *mobilize*. In a country which has had direct experience of fascism (and Stalinism) it is perhaps still necessary to explain, or to explain again, what that means—namely, to make men more mobile than they are. As free as dancers, as aware as football players, as surprising as guerillas. Anyone who thinks of the masses only as the object of politics cannot mobilize them. He wants to push them around. A parcel is not mobile; it can only be pushed to and fro. Marches, columns, parades, immobilize people. Propaganda, which does not release self-reliance but limits it, fits into the same pattern. It leads to depoliticization.

For the first time in history, the media are making possible mass participation in a social and socialized productive process, the practical means of which are in the hands of the masses themselves. Such a use of them would bring the communications media, which up to now have not deserved the name, into their own. In its present form, equipment like television or film does not serve communication but prevents it. It allows no reciprocal action between transmitter and receiver; technically speaking, it reduces feedback to the lowest point compatible with the system.

This state of affairs, however, cannot be justified technically. On the contrary. Electronic techniques recognize no contradiction in principle between transmitter and receiver. Every transistor radio is, by the nature of its construction, at the same time a potential transmitter; it can interact with other receivers by circuit reversal. The development from a mere distribution medium to a communications medium is technically not a problem. It is consciously prevented for understandable political reasons. The technical distinction between receivers and transmitters reflects the social division of labor into producers and consumers, which in the consciousness industry becomes of particular political importance. It is based, in the last analysis, on the basic contradiction between the ruling class and the ruled class—that is to say, between monopoly capital or monopolistic bureaucracy on the one hand and the dependent masses on the other.

This structural analogy can be worked out in detail. To the programs offered by the broadcasting cartels there correspond the politics offered by a power cartel consisting of parties constituted along authoritarian lines. In both cases marginal differences in their platforms reflect a competitive relationship which on essential questions is nonexistent. Minimal independent activity on the part of the voter/viewer is desired. As is the case with parliamentary elections under the two-party system, the feedback is reduced to indices. "Training in decision making" is reduced to the response to a single, three-point switching process: Program 1; Program 2; Switch off (abstention).

"Radio must be changed from a means of distribution to a means of communication. Radio would be the most wonderful means of communication imaginable in public life, a huge linked system—that is to say, it would be such if it were capable not only of transmitting but of receiving, of allowing the listener not only to hear but to speak, and did not isolate him but brought him into contact. Unrealizable in this social system, realizable in another, these proposals, which are, after all, only the natural consequences of technical development, help towards the propagation and shaping of that *other* system." [1]

THE ORWELLIAN FANTASY

3. George Orwell's bogey of a monolithic consciousness industry derives from a view of the media which is undialectical and obsolete. The possibility of total control of such a system at a central point belongs not to the future but to the past. With the aid of systems theory, a discipline which is part of bourgeois science—using, that is to say, categories which are immanent in the system—it can be demonstrated that a linked series of communications or, to use the technical term, switchable network, to the degree that it exceeds a certain critical size, can no longer be centrally controlled but only dealt with statistically. This basic "leakiness" of stochastic systems admittedly allows the calculation of probabilities based on sampling and extrapolations; but blanket supervision would de-

mand a monitor that was bigger than the system itself. The monitoring of all telephone conversations, for instance, postulates an apparatus which would need to be n times more extensive and more complicated than that of the present telephone system. A censor's office, which carried out its work extensively, would of necessity become the largest branch of industry in its society.

But supervision on the basis of approximation can only offer inadequate instruments for the self-regulation of the whole system in accordance with the concepts of those who govern it. It postulates a high degree of internal stability. If this precarious balance is upset, then crisis measures based on statistical methods of control are useless. Interference can penetrate the leaky nexus of the media, spreading and multiplying there with the utmost speed, by resonance. The regime so threatened will in such cases, insofar as it is still capable of action, use force and adopt police or military methods.

A state of emergency is therefore the only alternative to leakage in the consciousness industry; but it cannot be maintained in the long run. Societies in the late industrial age rely on the free exchange of information; the "objective pressures" to which their controllers constantly appeal are thus turned against them. Every attempt to suppress the random factors, each diminution of the average flow and each distortion of the information structure must, in the long run, lead to an embolism.

The electronic media have not only built up the information network intensively, they have also spread it extensively. The radio wars of the fifties demonstrated that in the realm of communications, national sovereignty is condemned to wither away. The further development of satellites will deal it the *coup de grâce*. Quarantine regulations for information, such as were promulgated by fascism and Stalinism, are only possible today at the cost of deliberate industrial regression.

Example. The Soviet bureaucracy, that is to say the most widespread and complicated bureaucracy in the world, has to deny itself almost entirely an elementary piece of organizational equipment, the duplicating machine, because this instrument potentially makes everyone a printer. The political risk involved, the possibility of a leakage in the information network, is accepted only at the highest levels, at exposed switchpoints in political, military, and scientific areas. It is clear that Soviet society has to pay an immense price for the suppression of its own productive resources—clumsy procedures, misinformation, *faux frais*. The phenomenon incidentally has its analogue in the capitalist West, if in a diluted form. The technically most advanced electrostatic copying machine, which operates with ordinary paper—which cannot, that is to say, be supervised and is independent of suppliers—is the property of a monopoly (Xerox), on principle it is not sold but rented. The rates themselves ensure that it does not get into the wrong hands. The equipment crops up as if by magic where economic and political power are concentrated. Political control of the equipment goes hand in hand with maximization of profits for the manufacturer. Admittedly this control, as opposed to Soviet methods, is by no means "watertight" for the reasons indicated.

The problem of censorship thus enters a new historical stage. The struggle for the freedom of the press and freedom of ideas has, up till now, been mainly an argument within the bourgeoisie itself; for the masses, freedom to express opinions was a fiction since they were, from the beginning, barred from the means of production—above all from the press—and thus were unable to join in freedom of expression from the start. Today censorship is threatened by the productive forces of the consciousness industry which is already, to some extent, gaining the upper hand over the prevailing relations of production. Long before the latter are overthrown, the contradiction between what is possible and what actually exists will become acute.

CULTURAL ARCHAISM IN THE LEFT CRITIQUE

4. The New Left of the sixties has reduced the development of the media to a single concept—that of manipulation. This

concept was originally extremely useful for heuristic purposes and has made possible a great many individual analytical investigations, but it now threatens to degenerate into a mere slogan which conceals more than it is able to illuminate, and therefore itself requires analysis.

The current theory of manipulation on the Left is essentially defensive; its effects can lead the movement into defeatism. Subjectively speaking, behind the tendency to go on the defensive lies a sense of impotence. Objectively, it corresponds to the absolutely correct view that the decisive means of production are in enemy hands. But to react to this state of affairs with moral indignation is naive. There is in general an undertone of lamentation when people speak of manipulation which points to idealistic expectations—as if the class enemy had ever stuck to the promises of fair play it occasionally utters. The liberal superstition that in political and social questions there is such a thing as pure, unmanipulated truth seems to enjoy remarkable currency among the socialist Left. It is the unspoken basic premise of the manipulation thesis.

This thesis provides no incentive to push ahead. A socialist perspective which does not go beyond attacking existing property relationships is limited. The expropriation of Springer is a desirable goal but it would be good to know to whom the media should be handed over. The Party? To judge by all experience of that solution, it is not a possible alternative. It is perhaps no accident that the Left has not yet produced an analysis of the pattern of manipulation in countries with socialist regimes.

The manipulation thesis also serves to exculpate oneself. To cast the enemy in the role of the devil is to conceal the weakness and lack of perspective in one's own agitation. If the latter leads to self-isolation instead of mobilizing the masses, then its failure is attributed holus-bolus to the overwhelming power of the media.

The theory of repressive tolerance has also permeated discussion of the media by the Left. This concept, which was formulated by its author with the utmost care, has also, when whittled away in an undialectical manner, become a vehicle for resignation. Admittedly, when an office-equipment firm can attempt to recruit sales staff with the picture of Che Guevara and the text *We would have hired him,* the temptation to withdraw is great. But fear of handling shit is a luxury a sewerman cannot necessarily afford.

The electronic media do away with cleanliness; they are by their nature "dirty." That is part of their productive power. In terms of structure, they are antisectarian—a further reason why the Left, insofar as it is not prepared to re-examine its traditions, has little idea what to do with them. The desire for a cleanly defined "line" and for the suppression of "deviations" is anachronistic and now serves only one's own need for security. It weakens one's own position by irrational purges, exclusions, and fragmentation, instead of strengthening it by rational discussion.

These resistances and fears are strengthened by a series of cultural factors which, for the most part, operate unconsciously, and which are to be explained by the social history of the participants in today's Left movement—namely their bourgeois class background. It often seems as if it were precisely because of their progressive potential that the media are felt to be an immense threatening power; because for the first time they present a basic challenge to bourgeois culture and thereby to the privileges of the bourgeois intelligentsia—a challenge far more radical than any self-doubt this social group can display. In the New Left's opposition to the media, old bourgeois fears such as the fear of "the masses" seem to be reappearing along with equally old bourgeois longings for pre-industrial times dressed up in progressive clothing.

At the very beginning of the student revolt, during the Free Speech Movement at Berkeley, the computer was a favorite target for aggression. Interest in the Third World is not always free from motives based on antagonism towards civilization which has its source in conservative culture critique. During the May events in Paris the reversion to archaic forms of production was particularly characteristic. Instead of carrying out agitation among the workers with a modern offset press, the students printed their posters on the hand presses of the École des Beaux Arts. The political slogans were hand-painted; stencils would certainly have made it possible to produce them *en masse,* but it would have offended the creative imagination of the authors. The ability to make proper strategic use of the most advanced media was lacking. It was not the radio headquarters that were seized by the rebels, but the Odéon Theatre, steeped in tradition.

The obverse of this fear of contact with the media is the fascination they exert on left-wing movements in the great cities. On the one hand, the comrades take refuge in outdated forms of communication and esoteric arts and crafts instead of occupying themselves with the contradiction between the present constitution of the media and their revolutionary potential; on the other hand, they cannot escape from the consciousness industry's program or from its esthetic. This leads, subjectively, to a split between a puritanical view of political action and the area of private "leisure"; objectively, it leads to a split between politically active groups and subcultural groups.

In Western Europe the socialist movement mainly addresses itself to a public of converts through newspapers and journals which are exclusive in terms of language, content, and form. These newssheets presuppose a structure of party members and sympathizers and a situation, where the media are concerned, that roughly corresponds to the historical situation in 1900; they are obviously fixated on the *Iskra* model. Presumably the people who produce them listen to the Rolling Stones, watch occupations and strikes on television, and go to the cinema to see a Western or a Godard; only in their capacity as producers do they make an exception, and, in their analyses, the whole media sector is reduced to the slogan of "manipulation." Every foray into this territory is regarded from the start with suspicion as a step towards integration. This suspicion is not unjustified; it can however also mask one's own ambivalence and insecurity. Fear of being swallowed up by the system is a sign of weakness; it presupposes that capitalism could overcome any contradiction—a conviction which can easily be refuted historically and is theoretically untenable.

If the socialist movement writes off the new productive forces of the consciousness industry and relegates work on the media to a subculture, then we have a vicious circle. For the Underground may be increasingly aware of the technical and esthetic possibilities of the disc, of videotape, of the electronic camera, and so on, and is systematically exploring the terrain, but it has no political viewpoint of its own and therefore mostly falls a helpless victim to commercialism. The politically active groups then point to such cases with smug *Schadenfreude*. A process of unlearning is the result and both sides are the losers. Capitalism alone benefits from the Left's antagonism to the media, as it does from the depoliticization of the counterculture.

DEMOCRATIC MANIPULATION

5. Manipulation—etymologically, "handling"—means technical treatment of a given material with a particular goal in mind. When the technical intervention is of immediate social relevance, then manipulation is a political act. In the case of the media industry, that is by definition the case.

Thus every use of the media presupposes manipulation. The most elementary processes in media production, from the choice of the medium itself to shooting, cutting, synchronization, dubbing, right up to distribution, are all operations carried out on the raw material. There is no such thing as unmanipulated writing, filming, or broadcasting. The question is therefore not whether the media are manipulated, but who manipulates them. A revolutionary plan should not require the manipulators to disappear; on the contrary, it must make everyone a manipulator.

All technical manipulations are potentially dangerous; the manipulation of the media cannot be countered, however, by old or new forms of censorship, but only by direct social control, that is to say, by the mass of the people, who will have become productive. To this end, the elimination of capitalistic property relationships is a necessary but by no means sufficient condition. There have been no historical examples up until now of the mass self-regulating learning process which is made possible by the electronic media. The Communists' fear of releasing this potential, of the mobilizing capabilities of the media, of the interaction of free producers, is one of the main reasons why even in the socialist countries, the old bourgeois culture, greatly disguised and distorted but structurally intact, continues to hold sway.

As a historical explanation, it may be pointed out that the consciousness industry in Russia at the time of the October Revolution was extraordinarily backward; their productive capacity has grown enormously since then, but the productive relationships have been artificially preserved, often by force. Then, as now, a primitively edited press, books, and theater were the key media in the Soviet Union. The development of radio, film, and television is politically arrested. Foreign stations like the BBC, the Voice of America, and the *Deutschland Welle,* therefore, not only find listeners, but are received with almost boundless faith. Archaic media like the handwritten pamphlet and poems orally transmitted play an important role.

6. The new media are egalitarian in structure. Anyone can take part in them by a simple switching process. The programs themselves are not material things and can be reproduced at will. In this sense the electronic media are entirely different from the older media like the book or the easel painting, the exclusive class character of which is obvious. Television programs for privileged groups are certainly technically conceivable—closed-circuit television—but run counter to the structure. Potentially, the new media do away with all educational privileges and thereby with the cultural monopoly of the bourgeois intelligentsia. This is one of the reasons for the intelligentsia's resentment against the new industry. As for the "spirit" which they are endeavoring to defend against "depersonalization" and "mass culture," the sooner they abandon it the better.

PROPERTIES OF THE NEW MEDIA

7. The new media are orientated towards action, not contemplation; towards the present, not tradition. Their attitude to time is completely opposed to that of bourgeois culture, which aspires to possession, that is to extension in time, best of all, to eternity. The media produce no objects that can be hoarded and auctioned. They do away completely with "intellectual property" and liquidate the "heritage," that is to say, the class-specific handing-on of nonmaterial capital.

That does not mean to say that they have no history or that they contribute to the loss of historical consciousness. On the contrary, they make it possible for the first time to record historical material so that it can be reproduced at will. By making this material available for present-day purposes, they make it obvious to anyone using it that the writing of history is always manipulation. But the memory they hold in readiness is not the preserve of a scholarly caste. It is social. The banked information is accessible to anyone, and this accessibility is as instantaneous as its recording. It suffices to compare the model of a private library with that of a socialized data bank to recognize the structural difference between the two systems.

8. It is wrong to regard media equipment as mere means of consumption. It is always, in principle, also means of production and, indeed, since it is in the hands of the masses, socialized means of production. The contradiction between producers and consumers is not inherent in the electronic media; on the contrary, it has to be artificially reinforced by economic and administrative measures.

An early example of this is provided by the difference between telegraph and telephone. Whereas the former, to this day, has remained in the hands of a bureaucratic institution which can scan and file every text transmitted, the telephone is directly accessible to all users. With the aid of conference circuits, it can even make possible collective intervention in a discussion by physically remote groups.

On the other hand, those auditory and visual means of communication which rely on "wireless" are still subject to state control (legislation on wireless installations). In the face of technical developments, which long ago made local and international radio-telephony possible, and which constantly opened up new wavebands for television —in the UHF band alone, the dissemination of numerous programs in one locality is possible without interference, not to mention the possibilities offered by wired and satellite television—the prevailing laws for control of the air are anachronistic. They recall the time when the operation of a printing press was dependent on an imperial license. The socialist movements will take up the struggle for their own wavelengths and must, within the foreseeable future, build their own transmitters and relay stations.

9. One immediate consequence of the structural nature of the new media is that none of the regimes at present in power can release their potential. Only a free socialist society will be able to make them fully productive. A further characteristic of the most advanced media—probably the decisive one—confirms this thesis: their collective structure.

For the prospect that in future, with the aid of the media, anyone can become a producer, would remain apolitical and limited were this productive effort to find an outlet in individual tinkering. Work on the media is possible for an individual only insofar as it remains socially and therefore esthetically irrelevant. The collection of transparencies from the last holiday trip provides a model of this.

That is naturally what the prevailing market mechanisms have aimed at. It has long been clear from apparatus like miniature and 8-mm movie cameras, as well as the tape recorder, which are in actual fact already in the hands of the masses, that the individual, so long as he remains isolated, can become with their help at best an amateur but not a producer. Even so potent a means of production as the short-wave transmitter has been tamed in this way and reduced to a harmless and inconsequential hobby in the hands of scattered radio hams. The programs which the isolated amateur mounts are always only bad, outdated copies of what he in any case receives.

Private production for the media is no more than licensed cottage industry. Even when it is made public it remains pure compromise. To this end, the men who own the media have developed special programs which are usually called "Democratic Forum" or something of the kind. There, tucked away in the corner, "the reader (listener, viewer) has his say," which can naturally be cut short at any time. As in the case of public-opinion polling, he is only asked questions so that he may have a chance to confirm his own dependence. It is a control circuit where what is fed in has already made complete allowance for the feedback.

The concept of a license can also be used in another sense—in an economic one; the system attempts to make each participant into a concessionaire of the monopoly that develops his films or plays back his cassettes. The aim is to nip in the bud in this way that independence which video equipment, for instance, makes possible. Naturally, such tendencies go against the grain of the structure, and the new productive forces not only permit but indeed demand their reversal.

The poor, feeble, and frequently humiliating results of this licensed activity are often referred to with contempt by the professional media producers. On top of the damage suffered by the masses comes triumphant mockery because they clearly do not know how to use the media properly. The sort of thing that goes on in certain popular television shows is taken as proof that they are completely incapable of articulating on their own.

Not only does this run counter to the results of the latest psychological and pedagogical research, but it can easily be seen to be a reactionary protective formulation; the "gifted" people are quite simply defending their territories. Here we have a cultural analogue to the familiar political judgments concerning a working class which is presumed to be "stultified" and incapable of any kind of self-determination. Curiously, one may hear the view that the masses could never govern themselves out of the mouths of people who consider themselves socialists. In the best of cases, these are economists who cannot conceive of socialism as anything other than nationalization.

A SOCIALIST STRATEGY

10. Any socialist strategy for the media must, on the contrary, strive to end the isolation of the individual participants from the social learning and production process. This is impossible unless those concerned organize themselves. This is the political core of the question of the media. It is over this point that socialist concepts part company with the neo-liberal and technocratic ones. Anyone who expects to be emancipated by technological hardward, or by a system of hardware however structured, is the victim of an obscure belief in progress. Anyone who imagines that freedom for the media will be established if only everyone is busy transmitting and receiving is the dupe of a liberalism which, decked out in contemporary colors, merely peddles the faded concepts of a preordained harmony of social interests.

In the face of such illusions, what must be firmly held on to is that the proper use of the media demands organization and makes it possible. Every production that deals with the interests of the producers postulates a collective method of production. It is itself already a form of self-organization of social needs. Tape recorders, ordinary cameras, and movie cameras are already extensively owned by wage-earners. The question is why these means of production do not turn up at factories, in schools, in the offices of the bureaucracy, in short, everywhere where there is social conflict. By producing aggressive forms of publicity which were their own, the masses could secure evidence of their daily experiences and draw effective lessons from them.

Naturally, bourgeois society defends itself against such prospects with a battery of legal measures. It bases itself on the law of trespass, on commercial and official secrecy. While its secret services penetrate everywhere and plug in to the most intimate conversations, it pleads a touching concern for confidentiality, and makes a sensitive display of worrying about the question of privacy when all that is private is the interest of the exploiters. Only a collective, organized effort can tear down these paper walls.

Communication networks which are constructed for such purposes can, over and above their primary function, provide politically interesting organizational models. In the socialist movements the dialectic of discipline and spontaneity, centralism and decentralization, authoritarian leadership and anti-authoritarian disintegration has long ago reached deadlock. Networklike communications models built on the principle of reversibility of circuits might give indications of how to overcome this situation: a mass newspaper, written and distributed by its readers, a video network of politically active groups.

More radically than any good intention, more lastingly than existential flight from one's own class, the media, once they have come into their own, destroy the private production methods of bourgeois intellectuals. Only in productive work and learning processes can their individualism be broken down in such a way that it is transformed from morally based (that is to say, as individual as ever) self-sacrifice to a new kind of political self-understanding and behavior.

11. An all too widely disseminated thesis maintains that present-day capitalism lives by the exploitation of unreal needs. That is at best a half-truth. The results obtained by popular American sociologists like Vance Packard are not unuseful but limited. What they have to say about the stimulation of needs through advertising and artificial obsolescence can in any case not be adequately explained by the hypnotic pull exerted on the wage-earners by mass consumption. The hypothesis of "consumer terror" corresponds to the prejudices of a middle class, which considers itself politically enlightened, against the allegedly integrated proletariat, which has become petty bourgeois and corrupt. The attractive power of mass consumption is based not on the dictates of false needs, but on the falsification and exploitation of quite real and legitimate ones without which the parasitic process of advertising would be redundant. A socialist movement ought not to denounce these needs, but take them seriously, investigate them, and make them politically productive.

That is also valid for the consciousness industry. The electronic media do not owe their irresistible power to any sleight-of-hand but to the elemental power of deep social needs which come through even in the present depraved form of these media.

Precisely because no one bothers about them, the interests of the masses have remained a relatively unknown field, at least insofar as they are historically new. They certainly extend far beyond those goals which the traditional working class movement represented. Just as in the field of production, the industry which produces goods and the consciousness industry merge more and more, so too, subjectively, where needs are concerned, material and nonmaterial factors are closely interwoven. In the process old psycho-social themes are firmly embedded—social prestige, identification patterns—but powerful new themes emerge which are utopian in nature. From a materialistic point of view, neither the one nor the other must be suppressed.

Henri Lefèbvre has proposed the concept of the *spectacle,* the exhibition, the show, to fit the present form of mass consumption. Goods and shop windows, traffic and advertisements, stores and the world of communications, news and packaging, architecture and media production come together to form a totality, a permanent theater, which dominates not only the public city centers but also private interiors. The expression "beautiful living" makes the most commonplace objects of general use into props for this universal festival, in which the fetishistic nature of the commodities triumphs completely over their use value. The swindle these festivals perpetrate is, and remains, a swindle within the present social structure. But it is the harbinger of something else. Consumption as spectacle contains the promise that want will disappear. The deceptive, brutal, and obscene features of this festival derive from the fact that there can be no question of a real fulfillment of its promise. But so long as scarcity holds sway, use-value remains a decisive category which can only be abolished by trickery. Yet trickery on such a scale is only conceivable if it is based on mass need. This need—it is a utopian one—is there. It is the desire for a new ecology, for a breaking down of environmental barriers, for an esthetic which is not limited to the sphere of "the artistic." These desires are not—or are not primarily—internalized rules of the game as played by the capitalist system. They have physiological roots and can no longer be suppressed. Consumption as spectacle is—in parody form—the anticipation of a utopian situation.

The promises of the media demonstrate the same ambivalence. They are an answer to the mass need for nonmaterial variety and mobility—which at present finds its material realization in private car ownership and tourism—and they exploit it. Other collective wishes, which capital often recognizes more quickly and evaluates more correctly than its opponents, but naturally only so as to trap them and rob them of their explosive force, are just as powerful, just as unequivocally emancipatory: the need to take part in the social process on a local, national, and international scale; the need for new forms of interaction, for release from ignorance and tutelage; the need for self-determination. "Be everywhere!" is one of the most successful slogans of the media industry. The readers' parliament of *Bild-Zeitung** was direct democracy used against the interests of the *demos.* "Open spaces" and "free time" are concepts which corral and neutralize the urgent wishes of the masses.

There is corresponding acceptance by the media of utopian stories: e.g., the story of the young Italo-American who hijacked a passenger plane to get home from California to Rome was taken up without protest even by the reactionary mass press and undoubtedly correctly understood by its readers. The identification is based on what has become a general need. Nobody can understand why such journeys should be reserved for politicians, functionaries, and businessmen. The role of the pop star could be analyzed from a similar angle; in it the authoritarian and emancipatory factors are mingled in an extraordinary way. It is perhaps not unimportant that beat music offers groups, not individuals, as identification models. In the productions of the Rolling Stones (and in the manner of their production) the utopian content is apparent. Events like the Woodstock Festival, the concerts in Hyde Park, on the Isle of Wight, and at

* The Springer press mass publication.

Altamont, California, develop a mobilizing power which the political Left can only envy.

It is absolutely clear that, within the present social forms, the consciousness industry can satisfy none of the needs on which it lives and which it must fan, except in the illusory form of games. The point, however, is not to demolish its promises but to take them literally and to show that they can be met only through a cultural revolution. Socialists and socialist regimes which multiply the frustration of the masses by declaring their needs to be false, become the accomplices of the system they have undertaken to fight.

12. SUMMARY.

Repressive use of media	*Emancipatory use of media*
Centrally controlled program	Decentralized program
One transmitter, many receivers	Each receiver a potential transmitter
Immobilization of isolated individuals	Mobilization of the masses
Passive consumer behavior	Interaction of those involved, feedback
Depoliticization	A political learning process
Production by specialists	Collective production
Control by property owners or bureaucracy	Social control by self-organization

THE SUBVERSIVE POWER OF
THE NEW MEDIA

13. As far as the objectively subversive potentialities of the electronic media are concerned, both sides in the international class struggle—except for the fatalistic adherents of the thesis of manipulation in the metropoles—are of one mind. Frantz Fanon was the first to draw attention to the fact that the transistor receiver was one of the most important weapons in the Third World's fight for freedom. Albert Hertzog, ex-Minister of the South African Republic and the mouthpiece of the right wing of the ruling party, is of the opinion that

"television will lead to the ruin of the white man in South Africa." [2] American imperialism has recognized the situation. It attempts to meet the "revolution of rising expectations" in Latin America—that is what its ideologues call it— by scattering its own transmitters all over the continent and into the remotest regions of the Amazon basin, and by distributing single-frequency transistors to the native population. The attacks of the Nixon Administration on the capitalist media in the USA reveal its understanding that their reporting, however one-sided and distorted, has become a decisive factor in mobilizing people against the war in Vietnam. Whereas only twenty-five years ago the French massacres in Madagascar, with almost one hundred thousand dead, became known only to the readers of *Le Monde* under the heading of "Other News" and therefore remained unnoticed and without sequel in the capital city, today the media drag colonial wars into the centers of imperialism.

The direct mobilizing potentialities of the media become still more clear when they are consciously used for subversive ends. Their presence is a factor that immensely increases the demonstrative nature of any political act. The student movements in the USA, in Japan, and in Western Europe soon recognized this and, to begin with, achieved considerable momentary success with the aid of the media. These effects have worn off. Naive trust in the magical power of reproduction cannot replace organizational work; only active and coherent groups can force the media to comply with the logic of their actions. That can be demonstrated from the example of the Tupamaros in Uruguay, whose revolutionary practice has implicit in it publicity for their actions. Thus the actors become authors. The abduction of the American ambassador in Rio de Janeiro was planned with a view to its impact on the media. It was a television production. The Arab guerillas proceed in the same way. The first to experiment with these techniques internationally were the Cubans. Fidel appreciated the revolutionary potential of the media correctly from the first (Moncada, 1953). Today illegal political action demands at one and the same time maximum security and maximum publicity.

14. Revolutionary situations always bring with them discontinuous, spontaneous changes brought about by the masses in the existing aggregate of the media. How far the changes thus brought about take root and how permanent they are demonstrates the extent to which a cultural revolution is successful. The situation in the media is the most accurate and sensitive barometer for the rise of bureaucratic or Bonapartist anticyclones. So long as the cultural revolution has the initiative, the social imagination of the masses overcomes even technical backwardness and transforms the function of the old media so that their structures are exploded.

"With our work the Revolution has achieved a colossal labor of propaganda and enlightenment. We ripped up the traditional book into single pages, magnified these a hundred times, printed them in color and stuck them up as posters in the streets. . . . Our lack of printing equipment and the necessity for speed meant that, though the best work was hand-printed, the most rewarding was standardized, lapidary and adapted to the simplest mechanical form of reproduction. Thus State Decrees were printed as rolled-up illustrated leaflets, and Army Orders as illustrated pamphlets." [3]

In the twenties, the Russian film reached a standard that was far in advance of the available productive forces. Pudovkin's *Kinoglas* and Dziga Vertov's *Kinopravda* were no "newsreels" but political television magazine programs *avant l'écran*. The campaign against illiteracy in Cuba broke through the linear, exclusive, and isolating structure of the medium of the book. In the China of the Cultural Revolution, wall newspapers functioned like an electronic mass medium—at least in the big towns. The resistance of the Czechoslovak population to the Soviet invasion gave rise to spontaneous productivity on the part of the masses, which ignored the institutional barriers of the media. (Details to be supplied.) Such situations are exceptional. It is precisely their utopian nature, which reaches out beyond the existing productive forces (it follows that the productive relationships are not to be permanently overthrown), that makes them precarious, leads to reversals and defeats. They demonstrate all the more clearly what enormous political and cultural energies are hidden in the enchained masses and with what imagination they are able, at the moment of liberation, to realize all the opportunities offered by the new media.

THE MEDIA: AN EMPTY CATEGORY OF MARXIST THEORY

15. That the Marxist Left should argue theoretically and act practically from the standpoint of the most advanced productive forces in their society, that they should develop in depth all the liberating factors immanent in these forces and use them strategically, is no academic expectation but a political necessity. However, with a single great exception, that of Walter Benjamin (and in his footsteps, Brecht), Marxists have not understood the consciousness industry and have been aware only of its bourgeois-capitalist dark side and not of its socialist possibilities. An author like George Lukács is a perfect example of this theoretical and practical backwardness. Nor are the works of Horkheimer and Adorno free of a nostalgia which clings to early bourgeois media.

Their view of the cultural industry cannot be discussed here. Much more typical of Marxism between the two wars is the position of Lukács, which can be seen very clearly from an early essay on "Old Culture and New Culture." [4] "Anything that culture produces" can, according to Lukács, "have real cultural value only *if it is in itself* valuable, if the creation of each individual product is from the standpoint of its maker a single, finite process. It must, moreover, be a process conditioned by the *human* potentialities and capabilities of the creator. The most typical example of such a process is the work of art, where the entire genesis of the work is exclusively the result of the artist's labor and each detail of the work that emerges is determined by the individual qualities of the artist. In highly developed mechanical industry, on the other hand, any connection between the product and the creator is abolished. *The human being serves the machine, he adapts to it.* Production becomes completely independent of the human potentialities and capabilities of the worker." These "forces which destroy culture" impair the work's "truth to the material," its "level," and deal the final blow to the "work as an end in itself." There is no more question of "the organic unity of the products of culture, its harmonious, joy-giving being." Capitalist culture must lack "the simple and natural harmony and beauty of the old culture—culture in the true, literal sense of the word." Fortunately things need not remain so. The "culture of proletarian society," although "in the context of such scientific research as is possible at this time" nothing more can be said about it, will certainly remedy these ills. Lukács asks himself "which are the cultural values which, in accordance with the nature of this context, *can be taken over from the old society* by the new *and further developed.*" Answer: Not the inhuman machines but "the idea of mankind as an end in itself, the basic idea of the new culture," for it is "the inheritance of the classical idealism of the nineteenth century." Quite right. "This is where the philistine concept of *art* turns up with all its deadly obtuseness—an idea to which all technical considerations are foreign and which feels that with the provocative appearance of the new technology its end has come." [5]

These nostalgic backward glances at the landscape of the last century, these reactionary ideals, are already the forerunners of socialist realism, which mercilessly galvanized and then buried those very "cultural values" which Lukács rode out to rescue. Unfortunately, in the process, the Soviet cultural revolution was thrown to the wolves; but this esthete can in any case hardly have thought any more highly of it than did J. V. Stalin.

The inadequate understanding which Marxists have shown of the media and the questionable use they have made of them has produced a vacuum in Western industrialized countries into which a stream of non-Marxist hypotheses and practices has consequently flowed. From the Cabaret Voltaire to Andy Warhol's Factory, from the silent film comedians to the Beatles, from the first comic-strip artists to the present managers of the Underground, the apolitical have made much more radical progress in dealing with the media than any grouping of the Left. (Exception—Münzenberg.) Innocents have put themselves in the forefront of the new productive forces on the basis of mere intuitions with which communism —to its detriment—has not wished to concern itself. Today this apolitical avant-garde has found its ventriloquist and prophet in Marshall McLuhan, an author who admittedly lacks any analytical categories for the understanding of social processes, but whose confused books serve as a quarry of undigested observations for the media industry. Certainly his little finger has experienced more of the productive power of the new media than all the ideological commissions of the CPSU and their endless resolutions and directives put together.

Incapable of any theoretical construction, McLuhan does not present his material as a concept but as the common denominator of a reactionary doctrine of salvation. He admittedly did not invent but was the first to formulate explicitly a mystique of the media which dissolves all political problems in smoke—the same smoke that gets in the eyes of his followers. It promises the salvation of man through the technology of television and indeed of television as it is practiced today. Now McLuhan's attempt to stand Marx on his head is not exactly new. He shares with his numerous predecessors the determination to suppress all problems of the economic base, their idealistic tendencies, and their belittling of the class struggle in the naive terms of a vague humanism. A new Rousseau—like all copies, only a pale version of the old—he preaches the gospel of the new primitive man who, naturally on a higher level, must return to prehistoric tribal existence in the "global village."

It is scarcely worthwhile to deal with such concepts. This charlatan's most famous saying—"the medium is the message" —perhaps deserves more attention. In spite of its provocative idiocy, it betrays more than its author knows. It reveals in the most accurate way the tautological nature of the mystique of the media. The one remarkable thing about the television set, according to him, is that it moves—a thesis which in view of the nature of American programs has, admittedly, something attractive about it.

The complementary mistake consists in the widespread illusion that media are neutral instruments by which any "messages" one pleases can be transmitted without regard for their structure or for the structure of the medium. In the East European countries the television newsreaders read fifteen-minute-long conference communiqués and Central Committee resolutions which are not even suitable for printing in a newspaper, clearly under the delusion that they might fascinate a public of millions.

The sentence "The medium is the message" transmits yet another message, however, and a much more important one. It tells us that the bourgeoisie does indeed have all possible means at its disposal to communicate something to us, but that it has nothing more to say. It is ideologically sterile. Its intention to hold on to the control of the means of production at any price, while being incapable of making the socially necessary use of them, is here expressed with complete frankness in the superstructure. It wants the media *as such* and *to no purpose.*

This wish has been shared for decades and given symbolical expression by an artistic avant-garde whose program logically admits only the alternative of negative signals and amorphous noise. Example: the already outdated "literature of silence," Warhol's films in which everything can happen at once or nothing at all, and John Cage's forty-five-minute-long *Lecture on Nothing* (1959).

THE ACHIEVEMENT OF BENJAMIN

16. The revolution in the conditions of production in the superstructure has made the traditional esthetic theory unusable, completely unhinging its fundamental categories and destroying its "standards." The theory of knowledge on which it was based is outmoded. In the electronic media, a radically altered relationship between subject and object emerges with which the old critical concepts cannot deal. The idea of the self-sufficient work of art collapsed long ago. The long-drawn discussion over the death of art proceeds in a circle so long as it does not examine critically the esthetic concept on which it is based, so long as it employs criteria which no longer

correspond to the state of the productive forces. When constructing an esthetic adapted to the changed situation, one must take as a starting point the work of the only Marxist theoretician who recognized the liberating potential of the new media. Thirty-five years ago, that is to say, at a time when the consciousness industry was relatively undeveloped, Walter Benjamin subjected this phenomenon to a penetrating dialectical-materialist analysis. His approach has not been matched by any theory since then, much less further developed.

"One might generalize by saying: the technique of reproduction detaches the reproduced object from the domain of tradition. By making many reproductions it substitutes a plurality of copies for a unique existence and in permitting the reproduction to meet the beholder or listener in his own particular situation, it reactivates the object reproduced. These two processes lead to a tremendous shattering of tradition which is the obverse of the contemporary crisis and renewal of mankind. Both processes are intimately connected with the contemporary mass movements. Their most powerful agent is the film. Its social significance, particularly in its most positive form, is inconceivable without its destructive, cathartic aspect, that is, the liquidation of the traditional value of the cultural heritage.

"For the first time in world history, mechanical reproduction emancipates the work of art from its parasitical dependence on ritual. To an ever greater degree the work of art reproduced becomes the work of art designed for reproducibility. . . . But the instant the criterion of authenticity ceases to be applicable to artistic production, the total function of art is reversed. Instead of being based on ritual, it begins to be based on another practice—politics. . . . Today, by the absolute emphasis on its exhibition value, the work of art becomes a creation with entirely new functions, among which the one we are conscious of, the artistic function, later may be recognized as incidental." [6]

The trends which Benjamin recognized in his day in the film and the true import of which he grasped theoretically, have become patent today with the rapid development of the consciousness industry. What used to be called art, has now, in the strict Hegelian sense, been dialectically surpassed by and in the media. The quarrel about the end of art is otiose so long as this end is not understood dialectically. Artistic productivity reveals itself to be the extreme marginal case of a much more widespread productivity, and it is socially important only insofar as it surrenders all pretensions to autonomy and recognizes itself to be a marginal case. Wherever the professional producers make a virtue out of the necessity of their specialist skills and even derive a privileged status from them, their experience and knowledge have become useless. This means that as far as an esthetic theory is concerned, a radical change in perspectives is needed. Instead of looking at the productions of the new media from the point of view of the older modes of production we must, on the contrary, analyze the products of the traditional "artistic media from the standpoint of modern conditions of production.

"Earlier much futile thought had been devoted to the question of whether photography is an art. The primary question—whether the very invention of photography had not transformed the entire nature of art—was not raised. Soon the film theoreticians asked the same ill-considered question with regard to the film. But the difficulties which photography caused traditional esthetics were mere child's play as compared to those raised by the film." 7

The panic aroused by such a shift in perspectives is understandable. The process not only changes the old burdensome craft secrets in the superstructure into white elephants, it also conceals a genuinely destructive element. It is, in a word, risky. But the only chance for the esthetic tradition lies in its dialectical supersession. In the same way, classical physics has survived as a marginal special case within the framework of a much more comprehensive theory.

This state of affairs can be identified in individual cases in all the traditional artistic disciplines. Their present-day developments remain incomprehensible so long as one attempts to deduce them from their own prehistory. On the other hand, their usefulness or otherwise can be judged as soon as one regards them as special cases in a general esthetic of the media. Some indications of the possible critical approaches which stem from this will be made below, taking literature as an example.

THE SUPERSESSION OF WRITTEN CULTURE

17. Written literature has, historically speaking, played a dominant role for only a few centuries. Even today, the predominance of the book has an episodic air. An incomparably longer time preceded it in which literature was oral. Now it is being succeeded by the age of the electronic media, which tend once more to make people speak. At its period of fullest development, the book to some extent usurped the place of the more primitive but generally more accessible methods of production of the past; on the other hand, it was a stand-in for future methods which make it possible for everyone to become a producer.

The revolutionary role of the printed book has been described often enough and it would be absurd to deny it. From the point of view of its structure as a medium, written literature, like the bourgeoisie who produced it and whom it served, was progressive. (See the *Communist Manifesto*.) On the analogy of the economic development of capitalism, which was indispensable for the development of the industrial revolution, the nonmaterial productive forces could not have developed without their own capital accumulation. (We also owe the accumulation of *Das Kapital* and its teachings to the medium of the book.)

Nevertheless, almost everybody speaks better than he writes. (This also applies to authors.) Writing is a highly formalized technique which, in purely physiological terms, demands a peculiarly rigid bodily posture. To this there corresponds the high degree of social specialization that it demands. Professional writers have always tended to think in caste terms. The class character of their work is unquestionable, even in the age of universal compulsory education. The whole process is extraordinarily beset with taboos. Spelling mistakes, which are completely immaterial in terms of communication, are punished by the social disqualification of the writer. The rules that govern this technique have a normative power attributed to them for which there is no rational basis. Intimidation through the written word has remained a widespread and class-specific phenomenon even in advanced industrial societies.

These alienating factors cannot be eradicated from written literature. They are reinforced by the methods by which society transmits its writing techniques. While people learn to speak very early, and mostly in psychologically favorable conditions, learning to write forms an important part of authoritarian socialization by the school ("good writing" as a kind of breaking-in). This sets its stamp forever on written communication—on its tone, its syntax, and its whole style. (This also applies to the text on this page.)

The formalization of written language permits and encourages the repression of opposition. In speech, unresolved contradictions betray themselves by pauses, hesitations, slips of the tongue, repetitions, anacoluthons, quite apart from phrasing, mimicry, gesticulation, pace, and volume. The esthetic of written literature scorns such involuntary factors as "mistakes." It demands, explicitly or implicitly, the smoothing out of contradictions, rationalization, regularization of the spoken form irrespective of content. Even as a child, the writer is urged to hide his unsolved problems behind a protective screen of correctness.

Structurally, the printed book is a medium that operates as a monologue, isolating producer and reader. Feedback and interaction are extremely limited, demand elaborate procedures, and only in the rarest cases lead to corrections. Once an edition has been printed it cannot be corrected; at best it can be pulped. The control circuit in the case of literary criticism is extremely cumbersome and elitist. It excludes the public on principle.

None of the characteristics that distinguish written and printed literature apply to the electronic media. Microphone and camera abolish the class character of the mode of production (not of the production itself). The normative rules become unimportant. Oral interviews, arguments, demonstrations, neither demand nor allow orthography or "good writing." The television screen exposes the esthetic smoothing-out of contradictions as camouflage. Admittedly, swarms of liars appear on it, but anyone can see from a long way off that they are peddling something. As at present constituted, radio, film, and television are burdened to excess with authoritarian characteristics, the characteristics of the monologue, which they have inherited from older methods of production—and that is no accident. These outworn elements in today's media esthetics are demanded by the social relations. They do not follow from the structure of the media. On the contrary, they go against it, for the structure demands interaction.

It is extremely improbable, however, that writing as a special technique will disappear in the foreseeable future. That goes for the book as well, the practical advantages of which for many purposes remain obvious. It is admittedly less handy and takes up more room than other storage systems, but up to now it offers simpler methods of access than, for example, the microfilm or the tape bank. It ought to be integrated into the system as a marginal case and thereby forfeit its aura of cult and ritual.

This can be deduced from technological developments. Electronics are noticeably taking over writing: teleprinters, reading machines, high-speed transmissions, automatic photographic and electronic composition, automatic writing devices, typesetters, electrostatic processes, ampex libraries, cassette encyclopedias, photocopiers and magnetic copiers, speedprinters.

The outstanding Russian media expert El Lissitsky, incidentally, demanded an "electro-library" as far back as 1923—a request which, given the technical conditions of the time, must have seemed ridiculous or at least incomprehensible. This is how far this man's imagination reached into the future:

"I draw the following analogy:

Inventions in the field of verbal traffic	*Inventions in the field of general traffic*
Articulated language	Upright gait
Writing	The wheel
Gutenberg's printing press	Carts drawn by animal power
?	The automobile
?	The airplane

"I have produced this analogy to prove that so long as the book remains a palpable object, i.e. so long as it is not replaced by auto-vocalizing and kino-vocalizing representations, we must look to the field of the manufacture of books for basic innovations in the near future.

"There are signs at hand suggesting that this basic innovation is likely to come from the neighborhood of the collotype." [8]

Today, writing has in many cases already become a secondary technique, a means of transcribing orally recorded speech: tape-recorded proceedings, attempts at speech-pattern recognition, and the conversion of speech into writing.

18. The ineffectiveness of literary criticism when faced with so-called documentary literature is an indication of how far the critics' thinking has lagged behind the stage of the productive forces. It stems from the fact that the media have eliminated one of the most fundamental categories of esthetics up to now—fiction. The fiction/nonfiction argument has been laid to rest just as was the nineteenth century's favorite dialectic of "art" and "life." In his day, Benjamin demonstrated that the "apparatus" (the concept of the medium was not yet available to him) abolishes authenticity. In the productions of the consciousness industry, the difference between the "genuine" original and the reproduction disappears —"that aspect of reality which is not dependent on the apparatus has now become its most artificial aspect." The process of reproduction reacts on the object reproduced and alters it fundamentally. The effects of this have not yet been adequately explained epistemologically. The categorical uncertainties to which it gives rise also affect the concept of the documentary. Strictly speaking, it has shrunk to its legal di-

mensions. A document is something the "forging"—i.e. the reproduction—of which is punishable by imprisonment. This definition naturally has no theoretical meaning. The reason is that a reproduction, to the extent that its technical quality is good enough, cannot be distinguished in any way from the original, irrespective of whether it is a painting, a passport, or a bank note. The legal concept of the documentary record is only pragmatically useful; it serves only to protect economic interests.

The productions of the electronic media, by their nature, evade such distinctions as those between documentary and feature films. They are in every case explicitly determined by the given situation. The producer can never pretend, like the traditional novelist, "to stand above things." He is therefore partisan from the start. This fact finds formal expression in his techniques. Cutting, editing, dubbing—these are techniques for conscious manipulation without which the use of the new media is inconceivable. It is precisely in these work processes that their productive power reveals itself—and here it is completely immaterial whether one is dealing with the production of a reportage or a play. The material, whether "documentary" or "fiction," is in each case only a prototype, a half-finished article, and the more closely one examines its origins, the more blurred the difference becomes. (Develop more precisely. The reality in which a camera turns up is always faked, e.g. the moon landing.)

THE DESACRALIZATION OF ART

19. The media also do away with the old category of works of art which can only be considered as separate objects, not as independent of their material infrastructure. The media do not produce such objects. They create programs. Their production is in the nature of a process. That does not mean only (or not primarily) that there is no foreseeable end to the program—a fact which, in view of what we are at present presented with, admittedly makes a certain hostility to the

media understandable. It means, above all, that the media program is open to its own consequences without structural limitations. (This is not an empirical description but a demand. A demand which admittedly is not made of the medium from without; it is a consequence of its nature, from which the much-vaunted open form can be derived—and not as a modification of it—from an old esthetic.) The programs of the consciousness industry must subsume into themselves their own results, the reactions and the corrections which they call forth, otherwise they are already out-of-date. They are therefore to be thought of not as means of consumption but as means of their own production.

20. It is characteristic of artistic avant-gardes that they have, so to speak, a presentiment of the potentiality of media which still lie in the future. "It has always been one of the most important tasks of art to give rise to a demand, the time for the complete satisfaction of which has not yet come. The history of every art form has critical periods when that form strives towards effects which can only be easily achieved if the technical norm is changed, that is to say, in a new art form. The artistic extravagances and crudities which arise in this way, for instance in the so-called decadent period, really stem from art's richest historical source of power. Dadaism in the end teemed with such barbarisms. We can only now recognize the nature of its striving. Dadaism was attempting to achieve those effects which the public today seeks in film with the means of painting (or of literature)." [9] This is where the prognostic value of otherwise inessential productions, such as happenings, flux, and mixed-media shows, is to be found. There are writers who in their work show an awareness of the fact that media with the characteristics of the monologue today have only a residual use-value. Many of them admittedly draw fairly shortsighted conclusions from this glimpse of the truth. For example, they offer the user the opportunity to arrange the material provided by arbitrary permutations. Every reader as it were should write his own book. When carried to extremes, such attempts to produce interaction, even when it goes against the structure of the medium employed, are

nothing more than invitations to freewheel. Mere noise permits of no articulated interactions. Short cuts, of the kind that Concept Art peddles, are based on the banal and false conclusion that the development of the productive forces renders all work superfluous. With the same justification, one could leave a computer to its own devices on the assumption that a random generator will organize material production by itself. Fortunately, cybernetics experts are not given to such childish games.

21. For the old-fashioned "artist"—let us call him the author—it follows from these reflections that he must see it as his goal to make himself redundant as a specialist in much the same way as a teacher of literacy only fulfills his task when he is no longer necessary. Like every learning process, this process too is reciprocal. The specialist will learn as much or more from the nonspecialists as the other way round. Only then can he contrive to make himself dispensable.

Meanwhile, his social usefulness can best be measured by the degree to which he is capable of using the liberating factors in the media and bringing them to fruition. The tactical contradictions in which he must become involved in the process can neither be denied nor covered up in any way. But strategically his role is clear. The author has to work as the agent of the masses. He can lose himself in them only when they themselves become authors, the authors of history.

22. "Pessimism of the intelligence, optimism of the will" (Antonio Gramsci).

Translated by Stuart Hood

Tourists of the revolution

The European Left manifests an arbitrary and ideological relationship to the socialistically governed countries with its discussions about revisionism and anti-revisionism, "accomplishments" and "deformations"; and anyone who pays close attention to these discussions often finds it difficult to localize the voices he hears—as though the speakers were ventriloquists from whom issued something like a socialist *Weltgeist*. When such a dislocation occurs, the fabric of the conversation is deprived of something that requires foremost consideration: the role of the observer that devolves on the Western Left with respect to those countries where socialism has found—if not its realization—at least serious attempts in that direction.

No matter what attitude or position one takes toward these countries—and they run the gamut from blind identification to vitriolic dislike—the verdicts are invariably reached *from the outside*. No one who returns from a sojourn in socialism is a genuine part of the process he tries to describe. Neither voluntary commitment, nor the degree of solidarity with which one behaves, no propaganda action, no walk through the cane fields and schools, factories and mines, not to mention a few moments at the lectern or a quick handshake with the leader of the revolution, can deceive about that fact.

The less the traveler understands this and the less he questions his own position, the greater and more justified will be the animosity that the voyager into socialism encounters from the very onset—from both sides. Such as in these lines:

THE TRAVELERS

They come in the clothes of the affluent society,
a thorn in whose side they are, whose "unreliable elements,"
fitted out with academic titles,
writing books for the departments of sociology
of the best universities
(which underwrite the cost).
They get their visas in a jiffy,
are informed about anti-war campaigns,
about protests against the Vietnam war, in short:
they are treading the righteous path of history.
While they lounge in the shiny seats
of the international airports,
each flight they take an illegal act,
they feel pleasantly subversive,
their conscience is clean.
They are the comfortable travelers of the wave of the future,
with Rolleiflex cameras, perfectly suited
for the tropical light,
for underdevelopment;
with information charts for objective interviews,
if, however (of course), something less than impartial,
for they love the struggle,
the guerillas,
the zafras,
the hardships of life,
the vulgar Spanish of the natives.

After two or three weeks
(that's the maximum)
they write books about guerillas
or the Cuban national character,
about the hardships of life or
the vulgar Spanish of the natives.

Provided with systems, with methods,
they are obviously frustrated
by the missing sexual freedom in Cuba,
by the unfortunate puritanism of the revolution,

and they define that state of affairs
with honest melancholy
as the abyss between theory and practice.
In private (not in their book or at the round table)
they admit that they cut more cane
than the best machetero (those guys made fiesta all day).
These fourteen-day heroes declare
that the people in the inns want to dance,
that the intellectuals (completely depoliticized)
are still able to write poetry;
the night before their flight back, lying next to their women,
they believe
they have developed supernatural muscles.
They go at it like blacks, as though they were depraved.
The girls, pregnant every five years,
are delirious with these unaccustomed husbands,
now insatiable.
At home they look at slides
that show the family hero
surrounded by natives, fraternally embraced (...)

Herberto Padilla[1]

The travelers whom Padilla describes bear the distinctive features of the sixties; and perhaps the only ones who can judge how accurate and appropriate his observations and arguments are are those whom they are aimed at. But the mistrust that manifests itself in his text is not of today's vintage, nor of yesterday's. It exists since the existence of two established social systems and it is encountered by anyone who moves more or less freely between the two. This mistrust has hardened in the course of the last fifty years. It contains layers upon layers of past experiences, the recollection of misjudgments that have long since become a tradition with the Left in the capitalist societies.

However, the phenomenon cannot be gotten rid of by rhetoric alone. (Padilla's text, too, contains its hidden ambivalence.) What makes a more precise investigation necessary are the objective effects that these journeys into socialism have had over the years. These effects, of course, have nothing to do with the significance of the individual travelers who were not up to the role they were asked to play, nor with the import of their (mostly superficial) observations and their (frequently threadbare) arguments. What lends these reports significance and why they continue to play a certain, though diminishing, role has to do with the isolation of the socialist countries from the outside world. This exclusion is one element in international class warfare and, depending on how that conflict has gone since 1917, it has assumed the forms of blockade, ostracism, military cordon sanitaire, "iron curtain," The Wall, and so on. This condition finds its administrative equivalent in travel restrictions, different forms of censorship, anti-emigration edicts and complicated permission procedures of all kinds. The extent to which these measures were made necessary by socialist transformations, how far they have become bureaucratically institutionalized and are politically superfluous are questions that cannot be investigated here; nor can they be resolved in principle or once and for all time.

In any event, the consequences are serious. The flow of communication between the socialistically governed countries and the outside world is disrupted. Socialism becomes an internal and secretive affair, only accessible to those who have the opportunity to peek behind the mystifying façade. Ignorance and manipulation become the rule. These consequences don't necessarily devolve primarily to the disadvantage of the class enemy. On the contrary: the governments and monopolies of the capitalist world have news and spy services that are in a position to make up the information deficit. On the other hand, the Left is thrown back on anachronistic forms of communication if it is dissatisfied with the information and deformation provided by the bourgeois media. Among these surrogates the trip, the visit, the eye-witness report play an important role. The sources of error of this kind of information nexus are self-evident, and we shall try to name them. Considered as a whole, it is paradoxical that the social-socialist movements in the West have been generally dependent on individual views when it came to finding out something about collective life and production procedures; that is, for information about huge industrialization processes they have had to rely on a pre-industrial messenger service. No wonder the wanderers frequently cut a ridiculous figure. The puny flow of information is scarcely their fault. It has objective causes.

Now that the old difficulties have not disappeared but have become surpassable, and every one of us can travel to the USSR almost at will, to Bulgaria, the DDR, and Czechoslovakia, the criticism of the travelers also turns against those who stay at home. A lack of curiosity is spreading among the West European Left that, at first glance, is astonishing and that requires an explanation. Year after year, many of the comrades go to Sardinia, to Greece, or to Amsterdam; however, they assiduously shun contact with the Hungarian or Ukrainian reality. These avoidance strategies, too, have their pre-history. Even during the thirties and forties many Communists preferred, if possible, to avoid the USSR, which they praised in their writings as the true home of the working class—even when this country was open to them at all times. For this, however, they had more concrete reasons than present travelers. Brecht, for example, stayed only a few weeks in the USSR during his trip from Finland to California, avoiding contact with Soviet reality as much as possible—evidently so as not to endanger himself. Today many comrades fear contact for other reasons. And sheer disinterest on the part of the politically active is probably not one of them. What those who remain behind are afraid of, rather, are their own illbodings. They don't even let it get as far as contact with the reality of the socialist countries so as not to endanger their own fragile convictions. That is not to say that the others leave their fears behind when they journey into socialism. On the contrary: the same concern that keeps some at home others drag around with them. It's part of their moral handbaggage. The inquisitive ones, too, have developed their defense mechanisms in the last fifty years—to soften the shock when a purely imagined reality encounters an historical one. The first to characterize this operation was Lev Trotzky:

"Today the book market of all civilized countries overflows with books on the Soviet Union. . . . The literature which is dictated by blind hatred assumes an increasingly smaller proportion; a considerable part of the new works on the Soviet Union on the other hand, are acquiring an increasingly benign if not enchanted air. . . . The publications of the 'Friends of the Soviet Union' fall into three main categories. Dilettantistic journalism of a descriptive genre, more or less 'leftist' reports constitute the great majority of articles and books. Then we find publications of humanitarian, pacifistic and lyrical communism which, if anything, are even more pretentious. In third place stands the economic schematization in the spirit of the old-German lectern–socialism. . . .

"What unites these three categories despite their differences is their obeisance to the fait accompli and their preference for soporific generalizations. They are incapable of rebelling against their own capitalism, and are therefore that much more eager to support themselves with a revolution that is already subsiding. Before the October Revolution not one of these people or their spiritual ancestors seriously asked themselves in what manner or form socialism would realize itself. Therefore, it comes that much easier to them to acknowledge what they find in the USSR as socialism. This not only provides them with a progressive appearance, but also with a certain moral fiber which, however, does not commit them to anything. This kind of contemplative, optimistic, anything but destructive literature, which presumes that all troubles are over, has a very calming effect on the readers' nerves and therefore is readily accepted. In this way an international school, which might be called *Bolshevism for the enlightened Bourgeoisie,* or in a strict sense *Socialism for radical tourists,* is imperceptively coming into existence." [2]

Trotzky's analysis, however, leaves untouched one centrally important aspect of the matter: *the institutional side* without which the Tourism of the Revolution remains incomprehensible. Whoever overlooks this side sooner or later arrives at a moralizing attitude that fixes on the character of a single individual. All one finds out this way is that X is naive, Y corrupt, and Z a hypocrite. But this explains nothing and nothing is won by it.

The institutional basis of "radical" or "revolutionary" tourism is the *delegacija* system. *Delegacija* actually means nothing but delegation, but the word has acquired a special meaning in Russian and designates official travelers of all kinds, even if they appear by themselves or in small groups; and it is by no means necessary for these people to have been delegated by anyone.

The following elements—inasmuch as they affect travelers from outside the country—are what make up the system:

1) The *delegate* is not undertaking the trip on his own account. He is invited. Normally he does not pay his own expenses. He is a guest and is therefore under the aegis of the unwritten laws of hospitality. From a material viewpoint this arrangement can lead to corruption; from a moral viewpoint to a defusing of criticism.

2) The *delegate* has to deal with hosts who occupy a monopolistic position. Paid-for trips also exist in capitalist countries; governments, organizations and firms particularly like to invite journalists, a procedure, which is considered a normal aspect of public relations. But usually the traveler is not dependent on such invitations, he can also travel without them. In contrast, the invitation as a *delegate* was (in every) and is (in some) countries the only possibility of acquiring a visa, the local currency, a room and transportation.

3) Compared to the general population, the *delegate* is in every respect a privileged person. When there is a shortage he enjoys precedence over the natives; hotel rooms, seats in public transportation, cars and chauffeurs are reserved for him; during longer stays he is permitted to buy at special shops; admission to special events normally off-limits to others and considerable sums are often made available to him.

4) The *delegate* is always cared for by an organization. He isn't supposed to—no, he isn't allowed to—worry about anything. Usually he receives a personal guide who functions as translator, nanny, and watchdog. Almost all contact with the host country is mediated through this companion, which makes distinct the *delegate's* segregation from the social reality surrounding him. The companion is responsible for the traveler's *program*. There is no traveling without a program. The guest may express his wishes in this respect; however, he remains dependent on the organization that invited him. In this respect he is treated as though he were still under-age.

The combination of being spoiled and impotent is reminiscent of infantile situations. Such visitors' lack of self-sufficiency can reach utter helplessness; it seems as though this state of affairs meets with the approval of the responsible organizations. The socialist countries have institutions that specialize in this kind of work; they are usually called "Society for the Friendship with the People" or something on that order. But all other organizations—from State apparatus and party apparatus to the women's organizations—have sections that take care of official guests.

The *delegacija* system is a Russian invention. It has its beginnings in the early twenties, and one can't assume that it was the intention from the start to pull the wool over the foreigners' eyes and to put them in a position that would lead to an inevitable loss of contact with reality. Anyone who assumes this kind of conspiracy demonizes a complicated relationship by inventing a theory which doesn't even completely apply today when it has become difficult to distinguish between cynicism and experience. For even now a delegate who, say, goes to Hungary, Cuba, or the Georgian Republic, will encounter completely genuine expressions of hospitality, and the trouble people take on his behalf not only serves to shield him from reality but also to protect him from situations that he might be unable to handle by himself. This was even more the case during the Russian civil war; that is, during the periods when the system was being created and when it was nearly impossible for a foreigner to travel to Russia without running the danger of dying from hunger, freezing to death, or being shot.

But that is just one side of the coin. Also, one should not forget that no cheaper or more effective means for influencing the outside world has ever been devised than the *delegacija* system. That is certainly one reason why it has spread from Russia over half the world. A few early examples give proof of its effectiveness. The first report is from Victor Serge and refers to the year 1920.

"The II. Congress of the Communist International con-

tinued its work in Moscow. Foreign colleagues and delegates
lived in a hotel in the center of the city, the Djelovoi Dvor,
which is situated at the end of a long boulevard whose one
side consists of the white battlement-crowned wall of the
Kitai-Gorod. Medieval portals beneath one nearby old tower
lead to the Warvarka where the legendary house of the
Romanovs stands. From there we went to the Kremlin, a
city within the city, all of whose entrances have guards that
control the passes. The twin-power of the revolution, the
Soviet Government and the International, were meeting there
in the palaces of the autocracy, amidst the Byzantine churches.
The only city that the foreign delegates did not get to know
—and their lack of interest in this respect confused me—
was the living Moscow with its hunger rations, its arrests, its
filthy prison stories, its black-market façades. Luxuriously fed
amidst the general misery (although, in fact, one served them
too many rotten eggs), led through museums to exemplary
kindergartens, the delegates of world socialism gave the impression of being on vacation or traveling as tourists through
our wasted, besieged republic. I discovered a new form of
unawareness, Marxist unawareness. A German party leader,
athletic and full of optimism, said to me quite simply that
'the internal contradictions of the Russian revolution contain
nothing surprising' for a Marxist, and in that he was undoubtedly right, but he used that general truth as an umbrella to avoid the immediate appearance of reality—which
has its importance despite everything. The majority of the
bolshevized left Marxists assumed this complacent attitude.
For them the words 'Dictatorship of the Proletariat' magically
explained everything without their ever thinking of asking
where the dictatorial proletariat was and what it was thinking, feeling and doing. . . .

"All in all, the foreign delegates were actually a disappoint-
ing crowd that delighted in valuable privileges in a famished
country; they were quick to be enthusiastic but mentally lazy.
One saw among them few workers and many politicians.
'How happy they are,' Jacques Mesnil said to me, 'that they
can finally watch parades from the official rostrum.' " [3]

Franz Jung's following observations fall into the same period: "Hunger also left its mark at the headquarters of the International, the Hotel Lux. Almost the entire intellectual and political elite of Europe and the world that stood close to socialism was presented to the Kremlin via the Hotel Lux —invited guests of honor of the government, sympathizers who had been advised to make the trip to Moscow and leading members of various Communist parties who had been ordered to Moscow.

"In May 1920, the food supply system of Hotel Lux had broken down. The distinguished hotel guests sat at long tables in the spacious dining room but could get nothing except tea with which everyone could provide himself from the samovars, which stood about everywhere. Several times a day, at irregular intervals, large bowls with caviar were placed on the tables together with plates of lox, but no bread and no kasa. Anyone who took the time to wait with his tea was bound to get caviar and lox at some point during the day.

"The prominent guests were very indignant at that time, most of them because they had upset stomachs due to the caviar and lox. They mentioned among themselves that if they were at the head of the government of the victorious revolution the food supply would be better organized, especially in the quarters of the government guests such as the Hotel Lux—they would see to that. They talked about this from early in the morning till late at night, at tea before the steaming samovar, while waiting for the next bowls full of caviar and plates with lox." [4]

Seven years later the contradictions within Soviet society had become even more acute and the blindness of certain visitors assumed grotesque proportions: "All opponents of 1927 went to the end of their terrible road, each in his own way no matter whether they let themselves be constantly humiliated out of loyalty to the party or put up constant resistance out of loyalty for socialism . . .

"What a crass contrast to these men were the foreigners, famous writers, Communist delegates, liberal guests of high rank who celebrated the tenth anniversary of the revolution in Moscow at that time! And they gave us lectures on how to be clever! Paul Marion (the future undersecretary of state in Pétain's government), member of the central committee of the Communist Party of France, was scattering boulevard bon mots about Moscow, knew how to appreciate the young Russian women and tried to explain to me that we were utopian; he himself saw the mistakes of the Communist movement very clearly, but continued to support it because 'despite everything, it was the only force . . .' He was just an average Frenchman—without intelligence—who was primarily interested in always coming out smelling like roses. All in all: buyable. . . .

"I met Barbusse, with whom I was corresponding, in the Hotel Metropole, guarded by an interpreter–secretary (from the GPU) and supported by a very pretty secretary doll . . . I was coming from the overcrowded rooms of the suburbs, from which comrades disappeared every night. I saw their women whose eyes were much too red and clouded with fear for me to feel very indulgent toward the great official foreign guests who were coming on tour; besides, I knew who had been chased from the hotel to accommodate the great writer . . . Barbusse had a large emaciated and supple body topped by a small, waxen, hollow-cheeked face with suffering lips. Right away I had a very different impression of him, primarily concerned not to be pinned down to anything, not to see anything that might have pinned him down against his will, concerned to conceal thoughts that he wasn't allowed to express, evading every direct question, always elusive, with uncertain glances, describing curves in the air with his slim hands while uttering words such as 'depths,' 'breadth,' 'augmentation,' and all this so as to make himself in fact the accomplice of the stronger side. But since one didn't know yet whether the struggle had really been decided, he had just dedicated one of his books to Trotzky, but didn't dare visit him so as not to compromise himself. When I mentioned the repression he acted as though he had a headache, as though he didn't understand, as though he were rising to wondrous heights of thought: 'Tragic fate of the revolution, breadth, depths, yes yes . . . oh my friend!' With a kind of cramp in my jaw I noticed that I was facing the human incarnation of hypocrisy." (Victor Serge)[5]

Examples such as these would probably enable one to develop a comparative psychology of such "Friends of the Soviet Union" and other countries, as well as of their trusting listeners at home; however, so as to become politically relevant such an analysis would have to go beyond individual idiosyncrasies and search out the historically determined elements of the wishful thinking and their blindness to reality and their corruption. The point is not to discover that "man is evil," but why professed socialists let themselves be politically blackmailed, morally bribed, and theoretically blinded, and not just a few individuals, but in droves. Such a reckoning of course cannot confine itself to an investigation of the "Tourism of the Revolutionaries"; this phenomenon, after all, is only one of the symptoms.

Let us return to the objective, institutional side of the *delegacija* business. The last example contains a suggestion how the system developed between 1920 and 1927; that is, from its crude beginnings to a far-flung, highly differentiated apparatus. Henri Barbusse, after all, was not a comrade, no central committee ever sent him to Moscow to the Comintern. Although he scarcely represented more than himself, he was received like a State guest. Yes, it is questionable in what sense, if any, he even belonged to the Left; his social position, his habits, his actions, and thinking characterize him rather as a typical bourgeois intellectual. And this was what constituted his political usefulness to the Soviet leadership at that time. The greater the precision with which the socialist bureaucracies learned to calculate such tactical victories, the more far-reaching their attempts to utilize the "Tourism of the Revolutionaries" as part of their political purposes. Under such circumstances it was inevitable that the *delegacija* system becomes differentiated. Varying categories of visitors, running the gamut from reactionary journalists to deserving party members and ultra-leftist sectarians, were assigned to different organizations, fitted out with carefully graded privileges and then sluiced through the country. A renegade who is an expert in these matters describes how the system functions in practice:

"A free-lance writer ranked somewhere near the bottom of the hierarchy. However, I was not a simple free-lance; I had an "organisation"—the MORP—which, being affiliated to the Comintern, was situated somewhere in the middle range of the pyramid. Moreover, I was a Party member, which improved my grading; but only a member of the German, not the Russian Party, which lowered it. I also carried on me a letter from *Agitprop Ekki* (Department of Agitation and Propaganda of the Executive Committee of the Communist International) which again considerably improved my grading.

"Such 'to whom it may concern' letters serve as a kind of passport in the Soviet Union. It is on their strength that the citizen obtains his permits, his accommodation, ration card, and so on. Accordingly, these letters are very carefully worded and graded, to convey the exact degree of priority to which the bearer is entitled. Mine was a "strong" letter, signed by the head of *Agitprop Ekki,* Comrade Gopner, in person. It said that I was a delegate of the Revolutionary Writers' League of Germany, and that I was travelling under the sponsorship of the Comintern.

"On the other hand, I was also a bourgeois foreign correspondent, working for several important newspapers, and duly accredited as such with the Press department of *Narkomindyel,* the Ministry of Foreign Affairs. This placed me in one of the top grades on another side of the pyramid, as it were. It entitled me to accommodation in *Intourist* Hotels where such existed; to travel in the "soft class" on trains; and to buy my food at *Insnab,* the co-operative stores reserved for the diplomatic corps, the foreign Press and foreign technical advisers. I disliked availing myself of these bourgeois privileges, but as I was travelling alone through remote and famine-stricken regions of the country, it was often the only way of obtaining food and shelter.

"I was careful never to show my bourgeois, *Narkomindyel,* documentation at the Party offices and factories that I visited, nor to travelling companions, for the immediate result would have been to arouse distrust and suspicion. On the other hand, I never showed my Comintern letter to hotel managers, railway officials and co-operative store managers—it would have deprived me of the preferential treatment for bourgeois tourists who have to be humoured for reasons of propaganda. Such a double existence was not regarded as dishonourable. On the contrary, it reflected the basic dualism of "*Narkomindyel* line" and "Comintern line"—the two aspects of the Soviet Union as a respectable international power, and as a clandestine centre of the world revolution. To bear this duality constantly in mind was one of the first lessons taught to every Party member.

"Thus I travelled symbolically in two different guises, and literally with one set of documents in my right-hand pocket, another in my left-hand pocket. I never mixed them up, thanks to the simple memorising device that the Comintern was "on the left."

"Even so, it would have been impossible for me to travel alone without falling back on the help of the only organisation that functioned efficiently everywhere throughout the country: the GPU. In every railway station in the Soviet Union there was a GPU Commissariat which maintained a minimum of order in the chaos. The function of the "Station GPU" was not political surveillance, but to act as railway officials, travel agents and information centres for official travellers. When I got out of the train in a new town, I went straight to the Station GPU, presented my papers, and was provided, as a matter of routine, with those basic necessities which no individual traveller can obtain without the "organisation" behind him: a room or bed, ration-card, means of transportation. My sponsors were the Comintern and the Foreign Ministry, neither of which had branch offices in small places; so the Station GPU took me under its wing until it was able to hand me over to the care of the slow-moving local Party Committee or Government Guest House. In short, the Station GPU had none of the sinister associations of that notorious body, of which it formed a kind of administrative public-service branch. It was, as I have said, the only efficient institution throughout the country, the steel framework which held the pyramid together . . ." [6]

Between 1925 and 1939 a great number of European intellectuals went, like Koestler, on a search for the coming time. The enormous dissemination that the literature produced by these "Friends of the Soviet Union" enjoyed was due to a massive need for concrete utopias—which the Soviet Union seemed to embody at that time. These books were by no means solely designed for the proletariat inasmuch as it was organized within the Communist parties, but also, and even primarily, for the petit-bourgeois intellectuals and the new "middle class" of employees who felt that capitalism endangered their existence. What secured a broad public for the "Tourism of the Revolution," therefore, was its bourgeois traits. The more euphoric, the more welcome this literature was: its illusions, which seem defects to us, were perhaps the basis of its success.

Of course, this literature never dominated the field. Since we are dealing with the Left or "leftist" tourism we will disregard the flood of anti-Soviet hate literature that the West produced after the October Revolution. It goes almost without saying that the wars of intervention and the economic and political pressures found their ideological complement in the press, in books and in film, that capitalism did not forego a propagandistic counter-offensive. Yet the Left too, produced documents of disillusion and vehement criticism of Soviet conditions alongside the literature of illusion. Such testimony begins to appear occasionally as early as the twenties. Particularly the anarchists published early reports of their experiences that shed a critical light on developments in the USSR. Examples of this are the books by Rudolf Rocker (*My Disillusionment in Russia,* New York 1923), Alexander Berkman (*The Bolshevik Myth. Diary 1920–24,* New York 1925), and Emma Goldman (*Living My Life,* New York 1934). Of course, these reports were written at a time when the *delegacija* system was still unknown, and only a small minority of people took any notice of them.

The French–Romanian writer Panait Istrati was presumably the first apostate among the "radical tourists." As Honorary President of the Society of Friends of the USSR, he had been invited to attend the tenth anniversary of the October Revolution in Moscow and had been received like a State guest. He aired his disappointment in a report *Après seize mois en URSS,* which was published in 1929 in Paris. This report manifests the radical turn-about from one extreme to the other that is characteristic of the anti-Communist utterances of many former pilgrims. Not a single argument muddies the flow of Istrati's confessions; the newly found disgust is only the reverse of the former blind belief. It is just as helplessly emotional and politically ignorant: "History," Istrati states very calmly, "confronts the workers with the question not whether they want socialism in fifteen years but whether they want their freedom at once." [7]

Istrati's piece, however, was only a bumbling predecessor of an entire wave of critical reports and analyses that began to appear in the thirties against the idolization of Stalinist USSR. The most sensational of these nay-sayings was by André Gide.

This famous man joined the Communist party at the age of sixty-three and then participated actively in the fight that helped the United Front to a short-lived victory in 1936. That same year he traveled to Moscow as guest of the Soviet Writers' Union and from there through large parts of the Union. The two books, which he published after his return, *Retour de l'URSS* and *Retouches à mon retour de l'URSS* (both Paris, 1936 and 1937 respectively) had a bomblike effect. Within one year more than 100,000 copies were sold and there were translations into fifteen languages.

What happened to André Gide in Russia? Nothing but the same treatment that his predecessors had enjoyed and taken little notice of; except that Gide was not Barbusse— on the contrary: for the first time the *delegacija* system revenged itself on its inventors.

"And indeed what disturbed me most when I got there, was not so much to find imperfections, as to meet once again with the advantages I had wanted to escape from, the privileges I had hoped were abolished. Certainly I thought it natural that a guest should be received as well as possible and everywhere shown the best. But what astonished me was that there was such a gap between this best and the common lot; such excessive privilege beside so mediocre or so bad an ordinary. . . .

"And of course I see that without any actual attempt at corruption it may very well be advantageous for the Soviet Government to make the way smooth for artists and writers and for all who will sing its praises; but I also see only too well how advantageous it may be for the writer to approve a government and a constitution which favour him to such an extent. This at once puts me on my guard. I am afraid of letting myself be seduced. The excessive advantages

I am offered over there frighten me. I did not go to the USSR to meet with privileges over again. Those that awaited me were flagrant.

"And why should I not say so?

"I had learnt from the Moscow newspapers that in a few months, more than 400,000 copies of my books had been sold. I leave you to calculate the percentage of author's rights. And the articles so richly paid for! If I had written dithyrambs on the USSR and Stalin, what a fortune! . . .

"These considerations would not have restrained my praise; neither will they prevent my criticisms. But I confess that the extraordinarily privileged position (more so than in any other country in Europe) granted to anyone who holds a pen—provided he writes in the proper spirit—contributed not a little to open my eyes. Of all the workers and artisans in the USSR writers are much the most favoured. Two of my travelling companions (each of them had the translation of one of his books in the press) searched the shops for antiques, curiosities, bric-a-brac—something on which to spend the thousands or so roubles they had cashed and knew they would not be able to take away with them. As for me, I could hardly make any impression on an enormous balance, for everything was offered me gratis. Yes, everything; from the journey itself to my packets of cigarettes. And every time I took out my note-case to settle a hotel or restaurant bill, to pay an account, to buy stamps or a newspaper, the delightful smile and authorative gesture of our guide stopped me. 'You're joking! You are our guest, and your five companions too.'

"No, I had nothing to complain of during the whole course of my tour in the USSR, and of all the spiteful explanations that have been invented to invalidate my criticisms, that which tried to put them down to the score of personal dissatisfaction is certainly the most absurd. I had never before travelled in such sumptuous style. In special railway carriages or the best cars, always the best rooms in the best hotels, the most abundant and the choicest food. And what a welcome! What attentions! What solicitude! Everywhere acclaimed, flattered, made much of, feasted. Nothing seemed too good, too exquisite to offer me. I should have been ungracious indeed to repulse such advances; I could not do so; and I keep a marvellous remembrance of it all, the liveliest gratitude. But these very favours constantly brought to mind privileges, differences where I had hoped to find equality.

"When, after escaping with great difficulty from official receptions and official supervision, I managed to get into contact with labourers whose wages were only four or five roubles a day, what could I think of the banquet in my honour which I could not avoid attending? An almost daily banquet at which the abundance of the hors-d'œuvre alone was such that one had already eaten three times too much before beginning the actual meal; a feast of six courses which used to last two hours and left you completely stupefied. The expense! Never having seen a bill, I cannot exactly estimate it, but one of my companions who was well up in the prices of things calculates that each banquet, with wines and liqueurs, must have come to more than three hundred roubles a head. Now there were six of us—seven with our guide; and often as many hosts as guests, sometimes many more." [8]

Gide's criticism of Soviet society is based in many respects on thoroughly bourgeois premises, most distinctly where he laments the country's "uniformity" and its inhabitants lack the "personal touch." For example, when he notices that Soviet citizens "own little private property" and when this outrages him he strikes an involuntary comic note. Brecht made some comments on this subject at the time, comments which should give "radical tourism" something to think about—above and beyond the case of Gide.

"The French writer André Gide has enriched the great book of his confessions with a further chapter. A tireless Odysseus, he has provided us with the report of a new venture, however without being able to divulge on board which ship this report was composed and where this ship is traveling to.

"Everyone who watched what he was writing at the time when he was preparing his last mistake had to look forward with considerable apprehension to his departure for the new continent. He greeted it as an individualist, primarily as an individualist.

"He set out like someone who is looking for a new country, tired of the old one, doubtlessly eager to hear his own yelp of joy, but what he was really looking for was *his* new country, not an unknown but a known country, not one that others but one that he himself had built, and in his head at that. He did not find this country. It apparently does not exist on this planet.

"He set out far too unprepared. But he did not travel untouched. He did not only bring the dust on his shoes. Now he is disappointed, not about the fact that the country does not exist but about the fact that this is not his country. One must understand this: After his trip he was in a position to say: This land is like so and so, its people do this and that, I don't quite understand. He expected a verdict of himself, he was one of the crowd that looked expectantly at him. He probably lacked the intention from the very beginning to communicate what this land is like, but what he is like, and that didn't take much time, this booklet was written quickly. He sat down and wrote . . . 'Everyone's happiness evidently consists only in de-personalization. The happiness of everyone is only achieved at the price of the individual. To be happy you must be uniform.'

"Here he broaches the question about the well-being of the people, and he is right: there probably never was a regime which so calmly admitted as the criterium of its effect the question whether the people were happy, and that means the many. Gide recognizes their happiness, he describes it in many places in his book, but immediately doubts whether what looks like happiness to him is happiness; that is, what he himself always calls happiness. He saw happy persons, in great numbers, but they were 'de-personalized.' They were happy but they were uniform. They lacked nothing to be happy, but Gide lacked something. Thus he reaches no new insight about happiness except perhaps that it is a scarce commodity. The reality he saw did not warp his measuring rod which he brought and took back with him. He did not come back happy, but as a personality. Also, what he called personality he will go on calling personality; he saw one country which lacked it: one sixth of the earth.

"Well, he is a skeptic like so many great clerics. His skepticism of course is not very general, not directed to all sides, it is a particular kind of skepticism, namely that of his class, the bourgeois class.

"It is skeptical toward other classes. Toward the concept of personality, toward his own, thoroughly bourgeois, concept of personality he is not skeptical. Here people are living under completely new, unheard-of conditions, for the first time the masses are in control of the means of production, making it impossible for individuals to use their talents to exploit others. Perhaps those personalities decay which were formed under other conditions and new kinds of personalities begin to form, which are meant for other kinds of social work, with other differentiations? Such personalities he would not call personalities." [9]

Brecht's critique of Gide is marked by rationality and equanimity, something one cannot claim for the reaction of the Communist parties. From now until the end of his life they were to call Gide a hyena, a perverse purveyor of filth, and mixer of poisons. Rereading his books today one must admit, however reluctantly, that they have outlasted much of what his Marxist opponents put on paper at that time. Probably only the crassest fanatic would disagree with some of his observations about bureaucracy and repression, official mendacity, and the privilege business. Gide was certainly wrong in considering himself a Communist, certainly he was unschooled in theory and politically naive and his taking sides was sentimental. Still, his idealism did not keep him from publishing the following table in which the approved representatives of the Diamat simply couldn't develop any interest at all:

	MINIMUM & MAXIMUM INCOME	USUAL INCOME
Workers	from 70–400 rubles	125–200 rubles
Small employees	80–250 rubles	130–180 rubles
Domestics	50–60 rubles (of course including room and board)	
Middle-rank officials and technicians, specialists, and those in "very responsible positions"	300–800 rubles	
High officials, certain professors, artists, and writers	1500–10,000 rubles and more; some, it is indicated, receive between 20,000 to 30,000 rubles per month.[10]	

There is a very simple reason why Gide's yellowed critique is not only acceptable but still readable today: it is his complete solidarity. This solidarity with the Russian workers and farmers is colored by Protestant moralism and is not devoid of idealistic mist; yes, at times is so simple as to be awkward. Still, it provides the decisive criterium. It is this solidarity that distinguishes Gide's report from the tirades of the other disillusioned ones, that separates him once and for all from the anti-Communist filth of the cold war, as well as from the arrogant know-it-all attitude and the malicious gleefulness that survives in some writers of the Left to this day.

Of course, one cannot compare today's attitude quite that simply with those of yesterday. Much has changed since Gide's days also with respect to traveling in countries like the Soviet Union. The infrastructure has improved, tourism has become a firmly established social institution—above and beyond caring for State guests of the revolution. The Intourist Bureau, the football club, the Ministry of Foreign Trade, the Writers' Union—every organization today has its specialists who take care of the *delegacija* unobtrusively and routinely. The GPU no longer exists and to mention its successor is considered bad form as much on the part of the hosts as the guests.

The USSR also is no longer the favorite travel objective of "radical" or "revolutionary tourists." The interest of this peculiar and ambiguous group has fallen on younger revolutions, on the non-European transitional societies.

The goals have changed, but the objective as well as subjective mechanism has remained the same. What Gide wrote before his trip to the Soviet Union is still valid:

"The stupidity and insidiousness of the attacks on the USSR is largely responsible for our conducting its defense with a certain wilfulness. These yapping dogs will begin to praise the way things are going in Russia at the very moment when we will stop doing so, because their praise will only be for the compromises and slander, for the deviations from the original objective which abet the gleeful exclamation: 'There, you see!' " [11]

The objections which are meant to prevent any criticism of the socialist transitional societies have scarcely changed since Gide enumerated them in 1937:

"1) that the malpractices which I have pointed out are exceptions to the rule from which one shouldn't draw any conclusions (because one cannot deny them);

2) that in order to admire the present state of affairs one needs only to compare it to the previous one, the condition before the conquest (mean to say: before the revolution);

3) that everything I complain about has profound ontological reasons which I have been unable to fathom: passing temporary evils in view of an imminent and that much greater state of well being." 12

The sterile debate between the admirers and defenders is being continued at any price, even at that of solidarity with the peoples who are being discussed, inasmuch as there is any room left for them between arrogance and loss of a sense of reality. Trotzky's dictum is still valid: "What really hides behind the 'official friends'' animosity to criticism is not so much concern for the fragility of socialism as the fragility of their own sympathy for socialism." Here, then, a recent example of this state of affairs:

"*China after the Cultural Revolution* is what Maria Antonietta Macciocchi calls her reports; a more fitting title would be *Marie Antoinette in Wonderland*. For this book by an Italian Communist Party delegate tells us less about China (where the author traveled together with her husband, the foreign political editor of *Unita*) than it does about the petit bourgeois mentality characteristic of so many party intellectuals. Her blindness toward the situation at her place of work, her incomprehension of production relationships and of human and social costs entailed by them, and her typical admiration of the colorful and sensuous aspect of goods becomes evident from the description which the author gives of a silk weaving plant in Hangchow which produces 'fifteen color' Mao pictures in large series: 'The thousand machines are spinning briskly always in the same rhythm, and from the looms pour the great beards of Marx and Engels, the pointed muttonchops of Lenin, the face of Mao with his forage cap. Then the gobelins showing historical events: Mao at the proclamation of the 20th of May; Mao in a bathrobe before the famous crossing of the Yangtze. . . . The poems of Mao too are printed in black and white. . . . The factory has 1700 workers who work three shifts, day and night, to satisfy the demand.'

"We too have visited this factory. But we didn't only see the 'glowing colors' of the large and small Mao pictures. The workers are standing in dark places where one ruins one's eyes and are exposed to incredible noise. The day shift lasts 8½ hours, the night shift 6½ hours. Seven days of vacation per year. Fifty-six days maternity leave including delivery time. Staggered wages, premiums as work incentives, preferential treatment for the drafting teams as compared with the producers. The Communist delegate has heard and seen nothing of this. She doesn't lose a word over it. When we met her recently and asked her about this discrepancy she said vehemently: 'Perhaps you don't know Italian factories?' 'Of course,' we replied, we know them as well as American and Soviet factories; but it never occurred to us to claim that Italy, the USA or the USSR are socialist countries.

"For Macciocchi, on the other hand, China is an ideal socialist country which 'manifests an entirely new model of industrialization.' This is due to the fact that she spent less time in the factories than in the company of functionaries who took her to the best restaurants in Peking." [14]

It is no accident but the political consequence of such an attitude that the great majority of "radical tourists" assiduously ignore the true situation of the working class in the socialistically governed countries. This striking disinterest is only barely concealed by means of declamatory slogans. The usual visits to factories and kolchozes tend to meet the indifference of these visitors at least halfway. They cannot and are not set up to break through the social segregation of the guests, whose contact is limited to designated individuals from the functionary class and to foreigners who live in the same hotels. This umbrella is so effective that most of the political tourists don't have the slightest idea of the working conditions even after weeks or months in the host country. Ask them about wages and working hours, protection against unlawful dismissal, housing assignments, the number of shifts worked and the premium system, living standards and rationalization and usually they have no answer. (In Havana I kept meeting Communists in the hotels for foreigners who had no idea that the energy and water supply in the working quarters had broken down during the afternoon, that bread was rationed, and that the population had to stand two hours in line for a slice of pizza; meanwhile the tourists in their hotel rooms were arguing about Lukács.)

In any event, there are indications that the Western traveler's awareness of problems is increasing. More and more reporters try to dispense with the ideological veil their status foists on them. Of course, one is more easily blinded when it is a question of one's own privileges. Even where the political intent of these privileges goes undetected one senses them more and more as a moral scandal, and they become problematical at least in this respect, as in the following reflections by Susan Sontag who visited Hanoi in Spring 1968:

". . . Hence, the store to which we were taken the third day to get tire sandals and have us each fitted for a pair of Vietnamese trousers. Hieu and Phan told us, with an almost proprietary pride, that this was a special store, reserved for foreigners (diplomatic personnel, guests) and important government people. I thought they should recognize that the existence of such facilities is 'un-Communist.' But maybe I'm showing here how 'American' I am.

I'm troubled, too by the meals at the Thong Nhat. While every lunch and dinner consists of several delicious meat and fish courses (we're eating only Vietnamese food) and whenever we eat everything in one of the large serving bowls a waitress instantly appears to put another one on our table, ninety-nine percent of the Vietnamese will have rice and bean curd for dinner tonight and are lucky to eat meat or fish once a month. Of course I haven't said anything. They'd probably be mystified, even insulted, if I suggested that we shouldn't be eating so much more than the average citizen's rations. It's well known that lavish and (what would be to us) self-sacrificing hospitality to guests is a staple of Oriental culture. Do I really expect them to violate their own sense of decorum? Still, it bothers me.
. . . It also exasperates me that we're driven even very short distances; the Peace Committee has rented two cars, in fact—Volgas—that wait with their drivers in front of the hotel whenever we're due

to go anywhere. The office of the NLF delegation in Hanoi, which we visited the other day, was all of two blocks from the hotel. And some of our other destinations proved to be no more than fifteen or twenty blocks away. Why don't they let us walk, as Bob, Andy, and I have agreed among ourselves we'd feel more comfortable doing? Do they have a rule: only the best for the guests? But that kind of politeness, it seems to me, could well be abolished in a Communist society. Or must we go by car because they think we're weak, effete foreigners (Westerners? Americans?) who also need to be reminded to get out of the sun? It disquiets me to think the Vietnamese might regard walking as beneath our dignity (as official guests, celebrities, or something). Whatever their reason, there's no budging them on this. We roll through the crowded streets in our big ugly black cars—the chauffeurs blasting away on their horns to make people on foot and on bicycles watch out, give way. . . . Best, of course, would be if they would lend us, or let us rent, bicycles. But though we've dropped hints to Oanh more than once, it's clear they don't or won't take the request seriously. When we broach it, are they at least amused? Or do they just think we're being silly or impolite or dumb?" [15]

The only traveler I know who has thought the problem of "radical tourism" through to the end is the Swede Jan Myrdal. With a conscientiousness that makes a veritably puritanical impression compared to the usual sloppiness in these matters, he gave an account (in his book *Report from a Chinese Village,* written in 1962 and published the following year) of the circumstances of his trip and his own situation. His reflections, therefore, and their exemplary character justify a longer quote.

"We financed our journey to China and our travels in China with our own resources. We probably could have become 'invitees'; the Chinese suggested this to us on several occasions, when we spoke of reducing our expenses, and that we did not do so was less because we thought that we would be corrupted—I have never believed myself to be easily corruptible and I don't think that I change my opinions because of small economic gains—but I intensely dislike the international junkets, the pleasure trips at public expense. The big powers, the Soviet Union, the United States, China, France, Great

Britain, are all subjecting the writers of small countries like Sweden (and of each other) to well-intentioned economic pressure through different forms of free travel 'with all expenses paid.' Even if I don't think I would be corrupted, I'm against the whole tendency. It has a perverting influence on the intellectual morals of the writer, it runs counter to the free expression of ideas. I can't stop this tendency, but I can at least say no for myself. I distrust free-loaders whether they are capitalists, communists, liberals, conservatives, anarchists or just plain sellers of words. I have never liked being grateful to anybody. And I can't understand how the public—that after all pays for it—can put up with this spectacle of politicians, writers and sundry 'public figures' banqueting their way around the world on a spree of phrases.

"But as my funds were by no means unlimited and as there were, and are, few facilities in China today for the tourist with a slim pocketbook, this led to certain conflicts. . . . I'm not criticizing the Chinese; in every country in which I have lived I have had to take up a discussion with the bureaucracy in order to be left in peace to do my work. The Chinese officials were reasonable and it took rather less time to convince them than it has taken in many other countries; also there was no question of corruption. They followed their regulations and I wanted to have these regulations changed.

"One of the prerequisite conditions for travelling in China today is that you accept interpreters and guides. We were given ours by the Chinese People's Association for Cultural Relations with Foreign Countries. I will come back to the question of interpreters, but I just want to point out that you either accept this condition or you don't travel outside Peking, Canton, Shanghai—and more often than not, not even there. I don't like this. But it is a tendency that is spreading from country to country. Even in Sweden we are starting to take in 'invitees,' give them guides and see to it that they keep looking at what we want to show them. I'm disturbed by this tendency. It gives strength to my fears that we, all over the world, are moving towards a more 'supervised' form of existence. But in this case I could not just say no, find a third way out or shift the emphasis. Either I have my travel supervised—or I stay at home, quite probably supervised in one way or another even there. However much I dislike it, I have to accept this condition. . . .

"Our chief interpreter was Pei Kwang-li. She had come with us from Peking. She was the most flexible, the best linguist and the most hard-working of the interpreters I had come across in China. I had tried several interpreters before getting hold of her, and we had been working together for about two weeks when we arrived at the village. She was supposed to go back to Peking from Yenan and it was only after some quite hard discussion that I managed to take her with me to Liu Ling. She was of great help to me in the village. She was friendly and cheerful and interested in the work. I gathered that she was afterwards criticized for her work with me. When we came back to Peking, she went away on vacation and after that she was not so friendly, natural and relaxed as she had been during the month in Liu Ling. She later on—when the book was finished—interpreted for us during our trip to Yunnan and during that trip she was cold, formal, dogmatic and even (which in China says much) quarrelled violently with us on the grounds that we showed 'anti-Chinese' opinions. As our 'anti-Chineseness' was our opinions about toil and sweat and peasant hunger that she had understood so well in Liu Ling, I cannot explain this change in her behaviour otherwise than that she had through 'criticism and self-criticism' come to evaluate us and our work in a different way and change her opinions about our way of working. Because of this I got rather less information in Yunnan than I had hoped for.

"The authorities in Yenan were very eager that we should not sleep in the village. They promised to arrange for us to be ferried there and back every day. We wanted, of course, to live in the village, we even demanded to be allowed to do so. The 'Old Secretary' of the village strongly supported us. To him it was a point of honour. After some discussion the Yenan authorities were (with some reluctance) convinced of our point of view. (The reluctance can be interpreted in many ways, one of them is that the Yenan authorities wanted us to be as comfortable as possible. They probably wanted to be kind. It is not their fault that their kindness would have made this book impossible.) We then lived in a stone cave (normally the party secretary's office) and I worked in another (the brigade's conference-room). Since we lived in a cave in a village of caves and ate the village food and the whole time associated with the villagers, it would be easy to say that we lived as one of the people. But that would be a romantic and thus mendacious description of reality. We were the first foreigners to have lived in the village, and the village honour required that our cave should be whitewashed and that we should eat well. We lived considerably better than the villagers. . . . As a guest in a village you eat well, you also eat with a certain reverence, because you know that you are eating the fruits of the toil and sweat of the people around you. But you never say so to your hosts. There is pride in toil. There is nothing 'objective' about food in a poor peasant village. It does not come out of a tin, neither is it something you carry with you from the city. But I was not one of the villagers. And I was not living like a Chinese peasant. . . .

"The decision to have an upper limit to the interviews, i.e., not to continue far up in the bureaucratic structure above the village, was contained in the idea of the book itself. But first I had thought of including at least some representative from Yenan, who could give the slightly larger picture of the village in its setting. I even tried to make that interview and spent one morning in Yenan interviewing the local party secretary, a young man. Unfortunately he was too dogmatic, too official to be of any value. (And this is a typical problem all over Asia: the middle echelon of bureaucracy is mostly young and dogmatic and narrow-mindedly inexperienced. The old experienced peasants are illiterate, the bright young administrators are already high up and the old intellectual generation of revolutionaries or 'national figures' are slowly fading away.) I don't blame the young bureaucrat from Yenan. He ran true to type, but when he flatly stated: 'We have here in our part never had any difficulty, never committed a mistake, never made a fault and we have no problems today,' I broke off the interview with a few nice, pleasant phrases, and decided that he was not to be included in the book and that I had better go back to the village and talk with the peasants."

Despite the careful thoughts Myrdal has addressed to the problems that the "observation" of a transitional society creates, and as convincing as his report seems, he cannot provide us with a general solution to these difficulties. Such a solution not only presumes a different attitude on the traveler's part but also a change in the objective conditions. The *delegacija* system will not disappear until the isolation of the socialistically governed countries is overcome and until the foreigner's as well as the indigenous worker's freedom of movement has been guaranteed. When everyone is free to choose his own companion—or decide to dispense with him; when the infrastructure is sufficiently developed to insure lodging, transportation, and food for everyone who is underway, when the total dependence on guides and controlling institutions has vanished—then the *delegacija* business will not necessarily cease of its own accord, but dependency, bribery, segregation from the working population, reality loss, and uncritical ingratiation as well as the privileges that are its material substratum will become straitjackets that everyone who does not feel comfortable can discard.

Such a development is foreseeable, that is, as an unplanned and perhaps unwished-for but necessary complement of a policy of global co-existence—whose questionable sides, incidentally, are no secret. But to ascertain its positive aspects does not mean to capitulate to the two-dimensional theories of convergence so much in favor with bourgeois observers. However, it is thinkable that the Left in the West will not use the opportunities that are becoming manifest here. Little speaks for the fact that those who adhere to socialism in the West will take up the confrontation with the attempt to realize it. Now that the objective difficulties are decreasing and it is becoming less and less a question, in many countries, of endangering anyone by talking with them, now that traveling is ceasing to be an individual privilege, it should be possible to launch a massive attack on this overdue task which no one has performed as yet: the analysis of socialist societies or those that go by that name. Individual messengers cannot undertake such an investigation. We have tried to detect the reason for their failure. But whoever curses the "radical tourism" of the last fifty years in order to conceal his own disinterest will find it difficult to reply to the question that is put to him when he is having his beer, or at streetcorner meetings or at demonstrations, the question: "Why don't you go live in the East?"

Translated by Michael Roloff

POSTSCRIPT

Postscript

Hans Magnus Enzensberger was born in 1929 in Kaufbeuren, a small town in Bavaria. Although he has admitted to a bourgeois upbringing, it should be remembered that a childhood and adolescence of that kind in the Germany of the 1930s and 1940s frequently entailed certain deviations from the middle-class norm. Aside from air-raid evacuations, which were standard, Enzensberger also underwent a brief army apprenticeship in the *Volkssturm,* Hitler's kiddie-cum-geriatric corps, and served a stint as bartender and translator for the Royal Air Force while engaging in blackmarket activities for a livelihood —all at age sixteen. However, after this presumably hectic period his life reverted once more to a bourgeois schoolboy's existence, or perhaps it didn't. In any event, he spent the next nine years at various German and European educational institutions, and in 1955 received a doctorate for his thesis on the *Poetics of Clemens Brentano.* In 1957 his first book, of poetry, *In Defense of the Wolves*[1] was published and Enzensberger moved to Norway for two years. The years 1959–1960 he spent in Italy. There followed one year as editor for his German publisher, Suhrkamp Verlag, and a further two-year retreat to Tjöme in the Bay of Oslo. In 1963 Enzensberger visited the Soviet Union for the first time (he had already spent a Greyhound summer in the USA), and he received the Büchner prize, the initiation into the world of German literary prizes. His acceptance speech cannot be described as grateful. In 1964–1965 he lectured on poetics at the University of Frankfurt and then paid his first extensive visit to South America. Thereupon he changed his domicile to Berlin where he founded *Kursbuch,* a quarterly magazine in which a number of essays in these two volumes[2] first appeared. For several months during 1967–1968 Enzensberger held a fellowship at the Center for Advanced Studies at Wesleyan University, Connecticut, which he terminated midway in protest against the crimes the United States Government was committing against the people of Southeast Asia. His letter of resignation later appeared in *The New York Review of Books.* After a visit to the Far East, Enzensberger spent the better part of one year in Cuba. This sojourn eventually resulted in the documentary play *The Havana Inquiry* (Holt, Rinehart and Winston, 1974) and the fascinating dissection of the Cuban Communist Party in *Picture of a Party: Prehistory, Structure and Ideology of the PCC* (P&C).

It would be possible to enumerate further Enzensberger trips. For example, I could recount how the author and editor of this volume came within a month of meeting each other on the docks of Colombo, Sri Lanka, last year. But, besides being purely informational, the preceding list tries to make the not unimportant point that Enzensberger's life cannot be described as altogether settled—despite the obvious consistencies of his interests. As a matter of fact, it would be possible to claim that he is driven as much by nervous curiosity (though hardly of an indiscriminate kind), as by a critical spirit: he may easily be one of the most widely traveled writers in the world today. He is also one of Germany's linguistically most talented. The bibliography of his works, at the end of this volume, does not include a listing of his translations (from the English, Italian, Spanish, Swedish and Russian), nor the writers whose work he has introduced into Germany, and that includes a large body of writing from and about the Third World. While in Norway he appears to have wasted no time in introducing numerous twentieth-century writers to Norwegian readers.

It is as a poet that Enzensberger is known in the United States, through the mistitled collection *poems for people who don't read poems* (Atheneum, 1968). Some of his essays have appeared in *Partisan Review, New Left Review, Encounter*, et cetera. Yet it would be too restrictive to identify Enzensberger too closely either as poet or essayist or as a combination of the two. Beginning as a poet, Enzensberger has in fact become something like a one-man literary and political guerilla enterprise who (as the bibliography demonstrates) resorts to whatever form serves his purpose at a particular moment. His magazine *Kursbuch* consistently provides a partisan yet even-handed analysis of intellectual affairs and all affairs conceivably of interest to intellectuals. What also distinguishes *Kursbuch* is the concentrated focus of each issue, which guarantees longevity, and a canny ability to be in the news by providing genuine news. So Enzensberger is as much poet as essayist as editor as translator as librettist and literary as well as political catalyst and critic. He is an analyst as well as activist, and his trenchant analyses have become more activist with time; as someone combining these activities in one person Enzensberger is a unique figure on the contemporary German scene—the exception that proves the point about the division of labor.

It will come as no surprise, then, that these two collections comprise only a small part of Enzensberger's work. Yet I will not forgo the claim that they are representative of his thought, as it has evolved over more than a decade, and that they contain many of his best, most exportable and important essays.

One could scarcely claim that Enzensberger was ever a-political. But I think one can say that he drew the consequences from his growing political awareness—that private dissatisfactions are totally enmeshed with social afflictions—gradually, perhaps even hesitantly. A succinct illustration of this ambivalence from the period when Enzensberger was in semi-exile from Germany, before he settled in West Berlin (which enjoys its special status too), are these lines from the poem *man spricht deutsch,* from *landessprache* (1960):

"What am I doing here
in this country [. . .]
native but comfortless
absentmindedly I am here, [. . .]
settled in cozy squalor,
in this nice contented hole, [. . .]
in this murderer's den, [. . .]
where the past rots and reeks in the rubbish disposal unit
and the future grits its false teeth [. . .]
where things are looking up but getting nowhere [. . .]
this country divided from itself, a rent an inwardly divided heart
senselessly ticking, a bomb made of flesh,
a wet, an absent wound:
germany, my country, unholy heart of nations,
pretty notorious more so every day,
among ordinary people elsewhere . . ." [3]

Allowing for the obvious differences, it is difficult not to be reminded of an attitude familiar with some American exiles in the 1920s. Taking a retrospective glance at the now defunct *Gruppe 47*, a self-made shelter for German writers during the late 1940s and 1950s, the *Gruppe* now appears like something of a creative writing class in internal exile. Still, the *Gruppe* members were politically more aware, if not active, than their American counterparts of the same period who could generally be found in the academies. There may be an international parallel here. Enzensberger's ambivalence of the 1950s manifests the characteristic struggle in a literary sensibility between a traditional perception of literature and a perhaps equally traditional perception of social justice. This conflict too certainly has its tradition by now. How Enzensberger has resolved that conflict, or how it needs to be continually resolved, can be seen by comparing the dates of composition of his essays. Allowing once more for obvious national differences, one can see that some of the changes in his emphasis, his thinking and his procedures have undergone in the past ten years are not that different from what has happened to some American writers in the same period.

What is less apparent in collections such as these are the circumstances that produced each of the essays—here they suddenly find themselves together, barren of their context. Like Enzensberger's poems, they were written at very particular moments, in answer to very particular requirements. Many of these essays, as most of Enzensberger's work, testify to the willingness to grapple with the particular demands of a moment or, to put it more emphatically: to meet the shit head-on. Like poems (who ever has heard of an "impartial" poem?) they attest to a profound partisanship. And though Enzensberger would not hesitate to call himself a Marxist and Socialist, within the context of the West German political scene—as *Berlin Commonplaces* (P&C), which is absolutely essential to an understanding of the German extra-parliamentary opposition, makes quite explicit—Enzensberger can only be understood as a "radical constitutionalist."

The essay that may evoke the greatest resistance among American readers (and I say so because it provoked resistance in me) is *Commonplaces about the Newest Literature* (1968). Understanding the context will be helpful in this instance—and I shall try to sketch its two main features—but is unlikely to lessen the resistance. The discussion about the efficacy and need, if any, of literature in a time such as ours certainly has been much more pervasive and conducted in sharper as well as more acrimonious terms in Germany in the late sixties than it was in the United States during those years. First of all, this has something to do with the German literary situation, which is simply more clearly defined than the literary situation in this country. Also, it does not hold many surprises, or rather, it does not hold as great a *threat* of surprises as the American situation does. As interesting as quite a number of German writers may be, the general context is still *thin*. A parallel to this state of affairs, incidentally, can be drawn to the German and American underworld. One of the few surprisers and disrupters of the generally predictable context is Enzensberger himself.

The second factor that might be kept in mind is the general uneasiness about art that has been in evidence in Germany ever since the end of World War Two. The grimmest formulation of this uneasiness certainly emanated from T. W. Adorno, in 1949. Since that part of the formulation that is known has already become an old and misquoted chestnut, quoting it in full may redeem it:

"Even the most acute awareness of imminent doom threatens to degenerate into gibberish. Cultural criticism finds itself confronted with the last stage of the dialectic of culture and barbarism: to write a poem after Auschwitz is barbaric [not 'impossible' as the misquote usually has it], and this also corrodes the awareness why it has become impossible to write poems today. The critical spirit is no match for the absolute reification of the intellect [. . .] as long as the critical spirit remains in a state of self-satisfied contemplation." [4]

Some have said that literature never made the grand claims for itself that Enzensberger tries to demonstrate it can no longer fulfill, and that his disclaimer therefore does not take anything away from literature. As questionable as such a position may be historically, what counts is that the work of those who allocate a more modest position to literature shows unmistakable signs of the awareness of the lessened possible efficacy that they expect their work to have. One can of course also simply dismiss Enzensberger's premises so as not to develop lockjaw trying to crack that hard nut *Commonplaces about the Newest Literature*. Or one can do as Walt Whitman when faced with Emerson's criticism of his poetry: "Each point of E.'s statement was unanswerable, no judge's charge ever more complete and convincing, I could never hear the points better put—and then I felt down in my soul the clear and unmistakable conviction to disobey all and pursue my own way." [5] That is, to hope that foxy, unpredictable circumstance will once more deke out apparently inescapable reality.

The difference between the Enzensberger of 1962 and the Enzensberger of the late sixties also becomes apparent when one compares the ease with which he puts the concepts of Poetry and Politics through their paces in the essay of the same name, with the profound doubt about literature's ability to do anything about the state of self-satisfied contemplation. Also remarkable is the neatness with which that juggling act is finally resolved in the sentence: "The poem expresses in exemplary fashion that it is not at the disposal of politics. That is its political content." Or the equally neat formulation that sums up *Theory of Treason* (P&C), an essay that could go a long way to deprive those of their irrational power who try to befuddle us with claims of national security: "What is primarily secret is what is a secret and what is not; that is perhaps the actual State secret."

The Aporias of the Avant-Garde requires little comment on my part. Everything said on the subject still applies, at least in Germany.

It will be helpful to compare *The Industrialization of the Mind* (1962) with *Constituent of a Theory of the Media* (1970) (one of the few recent statements from the Left that may conceivably send a few shivers up the spines of those in power), to see some of the consequences that Enzensberger draws from his own positions.

Theory of Treason, Dreamers of the Absolute I & II, Pu-

petta or the End of the New Camorra, Reflections Before a Glass Cage (all P&C) were originally written as radio essays. Some of them are therefore more expository and less analytical.

I gather that the German Left feels that *Tourists of the Revolution,* the concluding essay in this volume, represents Enzensberger's swan song to their cause. It would be unfortunate if they were so Germanically dogmatic and not accept valid criticism.

In 1971 Enzensberger published *Gedichte 1955–1970,* which contained a number of poems written after *Commonplaces about the Newest Literature.* This came as something of a surprise to those who felt that Enzensberger had forsworn the writing of poetry altogether. These lines—

> "All these differences
> Between sleeping tablets and wake-amins
> Between leftist and rightist sluts
> Occasionally exceed
> My capacity to differentiate."

may explain why that has not been possible.

Michael Roloff
October 1973

Bibliography of the Works
of Hans Magnus Enzensberger

Major Book Publications in German:

verteidigung der wölfe. (Poems), Frankfurt 1957.
landessprache. (Poems), Frankfurt 1960.
Clemens Brentano. (Dissertation), Munich 1961.
Einzelheiten. (Essays), Frankfurt 1962.
blindenschrift. (Poems), Frankfurt 1964.
Politik und Verbrechen. (Essays), Frankfurt 1964.
Deutschland, Deutschland unter anderm. (Political comments), Frankfurt 1967.
Das Verhör von Habana. (Documentary Play), Frankfurt 1970.
Gedichte 1955–1970. (Poems), Frankfurt 1971.
Der Kurze Sommer der Anarchie (Documentary Novel), Frankfurt 1972.

Book Publications in English:

poems for people who don't read poems, translated by michael hamburger, jerome rothenburg and the author, new york, 1968 (Atheneum).
The Havana Inquiry, translated by Peter Mayer, New York 1974 (Holt, Rinehart & Winston).
Politics and Crime, translated by Michael Roloff, New York Fall 1974 (A Continuum Book, Seabury Press).

On Hans Magnus Enzensberger:

The best source for material on H. M. Enzensberger is a volume entitled *Über Hans Magnus Enzensberger,* edition suhrkamp 403, Suhrkamp Verlag, Frankfurt am Main, 1970.

Notes

THE INDUSTRIALIZATION OF THE MIND

1. This delusion became painfully apparent during the Nazi regime in Germany, when many intellectuals thought it sufficient to retreat into "inner emigration," a posture which turned out to mean giving in to the Nazis. There have been similar tendencies in Communist countries during the reign of Stalinism. See Czeslaw Milosz's excellent study, *The Captive Mind* (London, 1953).

2. Karl Marx, *Die deutsche Ideologie*, (I Teil, 1845–46).

3. A good example is the current wave of McLuhanism. No matter how ingenious, no matter how shrewd and fresh some of this author's observations may seem, his understanding of media hardly deserves the name of a theory. His cheerful disregard of their social and political implications is pathetic. It is all too easy to see why the slogan "The medium is the message" has met with unbounded enthusiasm on the part of the media, since it does away, by a quick fix worthy of a cardsharp, with the question of truth. Whether the message is a lie or not has become irrelevant, since in the light of McLuhanism truth itself resides in the very existence of the medium, no matter what it may convey: the proof of the network is in the network. It is a pity that Goebbels has not lived to see this redemption of his *oeuvre*.

4. The importance of the transistor radio in the Algerian revolution has been emphasized by Frantz Fanon, and the role of television in the political life of Castro's Cuba is a matter of common knowledge.

5. A good example of this instinctive sense of insecurity shared by the most entrenched political powers is offered by Senator Joseph McCarthy's lunatic crusade against Hollywood producers, actors, and writers. Most of them had shown an abject loyalty to the demands of the industry throughout their career, and yet no abnegation of their talents could free them from suspicion. Much in the same way, Stalin never trusted even his most subservient lackeys of the intellectual establishment.

6. Among those who blithely disregard this fact, I would mention some European philosophers, for example Romano Guardini, Max Picard, and Ortega y Gasset. In America, this essentially conservative stance has been assumed by Henry Miller and a number of Beat Generation writers.

THE APORIAS OF THE AVANT-GARDE

1. Where obscurity is mistaken for profundity, the elegant modifier *shallow* is usually held in readiness to describe enlightenment. In such a climate of thought, it may be needful to note that the concept of the progressive can do without any kind of roseate halo. It does not in the least presuppose optimism or the conviction that man strives—perhaps even under constraint!—for perfection. Whoever clings to such a belief is merely

negating a negation whose real effects can scarcely be denied in the teeth of the universally planned return to the Stone Age. Even the person who would stick to his guns and refuse to join the general regression seems to be straining forward against an escaping multitude; he functions as a troublemaker. Thus the concept of progress is an obstacle to those who practice regression.

2. *Wider den missverstandenen Realismus* (Hamburg: 1958).

3. That all classical writers, without any exception, bask in "health" goes without saying. The "heritage" from Homer to Tolstoy must serve as a bludgeon with which modern literature is given whatfor. But not only the illustrious writers of the past are recruited as witnesses for the prosecution; Lukács does not hesitate to put into the witness box the American popular novelist Louis Bromfield, who is good enough for him to testify against Proust.

4. This negligence takes its toll when Lukács writes, "Lenin repeatedly criticizes the sectarian point of view, as if something of which an avant-garde has become fully conscious could be taken over by the masses without further ado." So quickly, then, can a concept be cured of its ills, if party discipline demands it.

5. Brockhaus, *Konversations-Lexikon*, Vol. II, 14th ed. (Berlin: 1894).

6. Ibid., Vol. VII.

7. Vladimir I. Lenin, *Works*, Vol. XXXI (Berlin: 1958), p. 28 ff. Later incessantly reiterated.

8. Hence the amusing terminological difficulty that presents itself to all Marxists when they write about esthetic matters: avant-garde in the arts is to be damned, but avant-garde in politics is to be respected as authoritative.

9. This assertion is not a wholesale dismissal of whatever counts itself a part of the above groups, or is so counted by others. In this essay, the assertion can be elaborated only with regard to certain literary phenomena; an analysis of corresponding conditions in painting and music would go beyond its competence. Theodor W. Adorno has written about *"Das Altern der neuen Musik"* ("The Aging of New Music"). The essay stands completely by itself in contemporary music criticism for its acuteness and uncompromisingness. It is reprinted in the volume *Dissonanzen. Musik in der verwalteten Welt* (*Dissonances: Music in the Bureaucratic World*) (Göttingen: 1956). For the questions of nonobjective art, cf. Hans Platschek's excellent *Versuche zur modernen Malerei: Bilder als Fragezeichen* (*Essays on Modern Painting: Pictures as Question Marks*) (Munich: 1962).

10. *On the Road* (novel) (Hamburg: 1959) jacket copy; also *The New American Poetry, 1945–1960,* Donald M. Allen (ed.) (New York: 1960), p. 439. The sociological equivalent of esthetic indeterminacy is blind mobility, which is expressed already in the title of Kerouac's novel: change of locale as an end in itself; furthermore, a programmatically fostered promiscuity and obsession with the use of narcotics. The reverse side of this anarchic attitude is the strict code to which the members of the group must submit. There is stern differentiation between them and the outsiders, the so-called squares. To Norman Mailer, who has joined the movement, we owe a repertory of its principal rules in the form of a handy tabulation. These rules extend, among other things, to articles of clothing, philosophers, eating places, and jazz musicians that the hipster must favor.

This code is meant in utter earnest; Mailer will not be found guilty of the slightest irony. With equal determination, the group celebrates the secret language of its own invention, whose expressions act as passwords. Here no swerving is allowed, and "uninhibited word-slinging" becomes fixed ritual.

11. *material I* (Darmstadt: 1958). [The last two words in the German text are *ahne warumbe*.]

12. Ibid.

13. Hannah Arendt, *Origins of Totalitarianism* (New York: 1951).

14. *Movens. Dokumente und Analysen zur Dichtung, bildende Kunst, Musik, Architektur,* edited in collaboration with Walter Höllerer and Manfred de la Motte, by Franz Mon (Wiesbaden, 1960).

15. Exception must be made for the experiments Max Bense and his students have conducted by means of electronic computers. These experiments do meet scientific requirements. Concepts derived from combination and probability theories are here put to meaningful use. Whether the "stochastic texts" thus derived can be valid esthetic objects is a question of definition. Cf. *Augenblick (Instant),* Vol. IV, No. 1, Siegen: 1959.

16. Reprinted in A. Zervos, *Un Demi-siècle d'art italien* (Paris: 1950).

17. Cf. *Poeti futuristi,* Filippo Tommaso Marinetti (ed.) (Milan: 1912).

18. In his introduction to the anthology, *Lyrik des expressionistischen Jahrzehnts (Poetry of the Expressionist Decade)* (Wiesbaden: 1955).

19. Quoted from *Surrealismus. Texte und Kritik,* Alain Bosquet (ed.) (Berlin: 1950).

20. Hannah Arendt comments, in the work cited above, *Origins of Totalitarianism,* and particularly in the chapter on the mob and the elite, on the latent totalitarian strains in avant-garde movements. Of course, the occasional sympathies of the avant-garde with the totalitarian movements were thoroughly one-sided, as the example of the futurists in Italy and Russia demonstrates. Their love was not requited, and modern art, avant-gardist or not, was promptly lumped together and put on the index.

21. The details of this development are related by Maurice Nadeau in his *Histoire du surréalisme* (Paris: 1948); Amer. ed.: *The History of Surrealism* (New York: 1965).

22. Cf. Maurice Blanchot's *"Réflexions sur le surréalisme,"* in *La Part du feu* (Paris: 1949).

WORLD LANGUAGE OF MODERN POETRY

1. *Mon coeur mis à nu,* XLI. I am indebted to Paul Celan for drawing my attention to this passage.

2. What is said here is based on the preface to the *Museum der Modernen Poesie,* the first work to attempt a study of this problem.

3. *Europäische Literatur und lateinisches Mittelalter,* Chap. 1, (Bern: 1948).

4. Edited by Janheinz Jahn (Munich: 1954).

5. *Cf.* for example, the short but excellent anthology *The Poetry of*

Living Japan, by Takamichi Nonimiya and D. J. Enright (London: 1957).
Also the only German collection, *Der Schwermütige Ladekran* (St. Gallen:
1960).
6. Berlin, 1949.
7. Partially analogous problems also arise in painting. For these refer
to Hans Platschek's *Versuche zur modernen Malerei, Bilder als Fragezeichen* (Munich: 1962).

POETRY AND POLITICS

1. Plato, *The Republic,* in particular 377–401 and 559–608.
2. For this and what follows I am indebted to *Europäische Literatur
und lateinisches Mittelalter* by Ernst Robert Curtius (Bern: 1948). *Cf.* in
particular Chapters 8 and 9.
3. Lachmann 26, 10.
4. Ibid., 17, 6. For what follows *cf.* above all 19, 17; 17, 11; 31, 23; 26, 23;
26, 33; 28, 1; 28, 31.
5. From the milieu of the *Venezianische Epigramme,* Artemis-Ausgabe
II, 177 (Zürich: 1950).
6. *Sämtliche Werke und Briefe,* edited by Helmut Sembdner, Vol. I, 28
(Munich: 1961).
7. Written on July 31, 1898. Quoted from the jubilee edition, Vol. I
(Berlin: 1919).
8. Quoted from *Die Zeit* of February 9, 1962. Some critics have ques-
tioned the existence of Gerd Gaiser's and Hans Carossa's Hitler poems.
Gaiser's poem *"Der Führer"* can be found in his first book, *Reiter am
Himmel,* published in 1941; Carossa's poem is contained in a *Tornister-
schrift des Oberkommandos der Wehrmacht (Abteilung Inland). Zum
Geburtstag des Führers 1941. Heft 37;* the work bears the title *Dem
Führer, Worte deutscher Dichter.*
9. *The Republic,* 378; 391; 607.
10. Curtius, *op. cit.,* 169 f.
11. In the ironic *Lobgesänge auf König Ludwig* (1841), for example,
the moment the ruler's name is mentioned, the lines degenerate to the
level of a mediocre cabaret or beerhall joke.
12. The name Hitler appears in only two of Brecht's poems, in the
"Lied Vom Anstreicher Hitler" and in the *"Hitler-Choräle"* (Gedichte III,
p. 35 ff, Frankfurt: 1961). Both were written in 1933. Later Brecht consistently avoided the name and instead used paraphrases like *der Tromm-
ler* or *der Anstreicher.* (Cf. *op. cit.* IV., p. 10, 16, 100 etc.). The difference
is not superficial. Brecht's most effective poems on fascism avoid all allusion to Hitler (*Die Erziehung der Hirse,* Berlin: 1951).
13. The poems mentioned are to be found in the *Museum der modernen
Poesie* (Frankfurt: 1960).
14. In *Die Heilige Familie,* Chapters V and VIII (Frankfurt: 1845).
15. Draft of a letter to Margret Harkness in *Über Kunst und Literatur,*
Karl Marx and Friedrich Engels (Berlin: 1949).
16. Ibid. On *Marx, Engels und die Dichter,* the book with this title by

Peter Demetz (Stuttgart: 1959); it contains a comprehensive chapter on Lukács.

17. Georg Lukács, *Wider den missverstandenen Realismus* (Hamburg: 1958).

18. Two great exceptions are Benjamin and Adorno. Benjamin's treatise on *Der Begriff der Kunstkritik in der deutschen Romantik* (Schriften II, Frankfurt: 1955) and Adorno's essay *"Zum Gedächtnis Eichendorffs"* (Noten zur Literatur I, Frankfurt: 1958) could form the basis of a true understanding of German romantic poetry.

19. *Journeaux intimes.* "Mon coeur mis à nu." LXXXIII.

20. *Auswahl in sechs Bänden,* I. (Berlin: 1959).

21. *Fülle des Daseins,* p. 106 (Frankfurt: 1958).

22. *Ausgewählte Gedichte,* p. 49 (Frankfurt: 1960).

23. *Gesammelte Werke* III, p. 656 (Hamburg: 1961).

24. *The Republic,* 424. In accordance with the Greek notion, Plato conceives music to include what we would call rhythm and metrical figuration, as well as accent and phrasing. This is clear from the context; *cf.* in particular 398–401.

COMMONPLACES ON THE NEWEST LITERATURE

1. A number of publications from the last months should be mentioned in reference to these *Commonplaces.* Particularly worth mentioning are: *Kritik: Eine Selbstdarstellung deutscher Kritiker,* edited by Peter Bamm, München (Hanser), 1968. *Kürbiskern* 4/1968, Martin Walser, postscript to *Bottroper Protokolle,* by Erika Runge, Frankfurt am Main (Suhrkamp) 1968. Karel Teige, *Liquidierung der "Kunst,"* Analysen und Manifeste, Frankfurt am Main (Suhrkamp), 1968. The Breton quotes are from *The Second Surrealist Manifesto* of 1930. Régis Debray's letter is dated September 20, 1967, Camiri. The sentence from Walter Benjamin can be found in his *Versuche über Brecht.*

CONSTITUENTS OF A THEORY OF THE MEDIA

1. Bertolt Brecht: *Theory of Radio* (1932), *Gesammelte Werke,* Band VIII, pp. 129 seq., 134.

2. *Der Spiegel,* 20/10/1969.

3. El Lissitsky, "The Future of the Book," *New Left Review,* No. 41, p. 42.

4. *Kommunismus, Zeitschrift der Kommunistischen Internationale für die Länder Südosteuropas,* 1920, pp. 1538–49.

5. Walter Benjamin: *Kleine Geschichte der Photographie* in *Das Kunstwerk im Zeitalter seiner technischen Reproduzierbarkeit* (Frankfurt: 1963), p. 69.

6. Walter Benjamin: "The Work of Art in the Age of Mechanical Reproduction," *Illuminations* (New York: 1969), pp. 223–7.

7. Ibid., p. 229.

8. Op. cit., p. 40.

9. Benjamin, op. cit., p. 42.

TOURISTS OF THE REVOLUTION

1. Herberto Padilla, *Ausserhalb des Spiels* (Frankfurt am Main: 1971), pp. 113–115.

2. Lev Davidovic Trockij, *Verratene Revolution* (Frankfurt am Main: 1968), pp. 5–7.

3. Victor Serge, *Beruf: Revolutionär* (Frankfurt am Main: 1967), pp. 122, 169 ff.

4. Franz Jung, *Der Weg nach unten* (Neuwied: 1961), p. 169 ff.

5. Victor Serge, *op. cit.*, pp. 265–267.

6. Arthur Koestler, *Arrow in the Blue* (New York: 1970).

7. Panait Istrati, quoted from Jürgen Rühle, *Literatur und Revolution* (München: 1960), p. 402.

8. André Gide, *Retuschen zu meinem Russlandbuch*, in Reisen (Stuttgart: 1966), pp. 413–415.

9. Bertolt Brecht, *Kraft und Schwäche der Utopie*, in *Gesammelte Werke* VIII (Frankfurt am Main: 1967), pp. 434–437.

10. André Gide, *op. cit.*, p. 404. Gide is referring here to a pamphlet by M. Yvon, "Ce qu'est devenue la Revolution Russe."

11. *Nouvelle Revue Française*, March, 1936.

12. André Gide, *op. cit.*, p. 8.

13. Lev Davidovic Trockij, *op. cit.*, p. 8.

14. Umberto Melotti, in *Terzo Mondo* (Milano: March, 1972), pp. 93 ff. The book by Maria Macciocchi that he criticizes appeared in Milano in 1971 under the title *Dalla Cina, dopo la rivoluzione culturale*.

15. Susan Sontag, *Trip to Hanoi* (New York: 1969).

16. Jan Myrdal, *Report from a Chinese Village* (New York: 1965).

POSTSCRIPT

1. A bibliography of Enzensberger's major publications in German and English can be found at the back of this volume.

2. This selection will be followed within six months by the American publication of *Politics & Crime*, which is devoted to the topics that its title announces. Essays from this second selection referred to in this postscript will be marked (P&C).

3. From: *poems for people who don't read poems,* translated by michael hamburger and jerome rothenberg, atheneum, new york, 1968, © 1967 by Hans Magnus Enzensberger.

4. From: Kulturkritik und Gesellschaft, *Prismen* © 1955 by Suhrkamp Verlag Frankfurt am Main.

5. From: Boston Common—More of Emerson, *Specimen Days.*

Index